NEW Blueprint INTERMEDIATE

Brian Abbs & Ingrid Freebairn

Students' Book

Longman

Contents

Unit		Focus	Listening	Reading
Rapid review	6–13			
1 Nick, a student	14	Character presentation	Opinions on education	Nick, a student
2 Present simple and continuous	16	Grammar	Commercial for a TV series	
3 Shopping	18	Communication	Conversation in a music shop	
4 *Not allowed to/not supposed to*	20	Grammar	Theatre announcement	
5 Understanding boys	21	Reading		Understanding boys
6 Past simple and continuous	22	Grammar	Account of a theft	
7 A career in films	24	Topic	Story of an amusing incident	Banderas – International film star
8 Apologies	26	Communication	Conversations at a party	
9 *Used to/be used to*	28	Grammar	Students' opinions of Britain	
10 Cider with Rosie	30	Reading		*Cider with Rosie* by Laurie Lee
Check/Use your English/Progress test	32–35			
11 Angie, a motorcycle courier	36	Character presentation	People talk about social changes	Angie, a motorcycle courier
12 Future tenses: *going to* and *will*	38	Grammar	Telephone conversations about arrangements	
13 Requests	40	Communication	Noting a telephone request	
14 Ability and possibility: *can/could/ be able to*	42	Grammar		
15 Blackberries	44	Reading		*Blackberries*, a short story
16 First conditional and time clauses	46	Grammar	Radio interview with athletics trainer	
17 Sport	48	Topic	Sports commentaries	*Winning at all costs*
18 Checking information	50	Communication	Conversation in the street	
19 *In case*	52	Grammar	Travel advice	
20 Fever Pitch	53	Reading	Cup Final commentary	*Fever Pitch*, biography extract
Check/Use your English/Progress test	54–57			
21 Glenn, an American in Britain	58	Character presentation	Impressions of Britain	Glenn, an American in Britain
22 Present perfect simple and continuous	60	Grammar	A letter cassette (with personal news)	
23 Making complaints	62	Communication	Telephone complaints	Advertisements
24 *Make/do*	64	Grammar		Using dictionaries
25 Theatrical anecdotes	65	Reading		Jigsaw reading (theatrical anecdotes)

Contents

Speaking	Writing	Vocabulary	Discussion
		Word field: education	Private v state education Education systems
Personal interviews	Character description		
Buying things in shops	Dialogue	Revision of clothes and stationery items	
Dialogue outside a theatre		Restrictions, rules and regulations	
	Using linking devices: *both … and, as well as, neither … nor*	Adjectives of personal description and their opposites	The basis of sexism
Narrating past events	Account of an incident		
	Biography and autobiography using time connectors	Word formation: adverbs with *-ly* Word stress: adjectives and adverbs	
Family argument	Letter of thanks and apology	Idiomatic expressions	
Conversation about a student	Informal letter		Changing lifestyles Student life in Britain and the USA First impressions
	Guided composition: description of an interesting room	Compound nouns: furniture and fittings	Large families
		Noun formation (jobs and professions) with suffixes *-er, -or, -ist*	Sex roles in work Urban redevelopment
	Message for a noticeboard	Outdoor leisure pursuits	
Dialogue at a reception desk Conversation with a taxi driver	Note of explanation with a request		
Making and responding to requests Roleplay a parent/teenage situation	Formal letter of invitation	Time phrases	
	Dialogue (a quarrel)	Collocation: verbs of spoiling e.g. *scratch, stain, tear* and nouns	Difficulties of family relationships Growing up
	'Good running' guide	Parts of the body Sports training advice	
	Formal letter to a newspaper	Word field: sports and their locations	Corruption in sport The commercialisation of sport Attitudes to winning
Dialogue between friends	Paragraph using linking devices: *another reason is, also, finally*		Meaning and language Comparing languages
	Note of welcome and explanation		Planning for survival
		Word field: football	Ideal activities and outings
		Uses of verb: *to get* + adjective/past participle American and British English	The effects of mass tourism
	An informal letter		
Dialogue (complaining in a restaurant)	Formal letter of complaint		
		Special verbs: *make, do*	
		Word field: the theatre and performing arts	

Contents

Unit			Focus	Listening	Reading
26	The passive	66	Grammar	Description of an audition	
27	The USA	68	Topic	Opinions of the USA	The Empire State Building
28	Obligation and prohibition	70	Communication	Table manners in the USA	
29	Defining relative pronouns	72	Grammar		
30	How to be an alien	74	Reading	National stereotypes portrayed in jokes	
Check/Use your English/Progress test		76–79			
31	Eve, a jewellery maker	80	Character presentation	A silversmith talks about his work	Eve, a jewellery maker
32	Second conditional *if* clauses	82	Grammar	Discussion about perfect occupations	Assertiveness questionnaire
33	Polite requests for information	84	Communication	Radio interview	
34	*Have/get something done*	86	Grammar	TV rental situation	
35	Friday Dressing	88	Reading	Different 'images' of business people	Newspaper article about dress codes
36	Past modal verbs: *should have/ ought to have*	89	Grammar		
37	Ethics	90	Topic	A personal dilemma	The ethics of friendship
38	Explanation and clarification	92	Communication	Conversation at a college	
39	Past modal verbs: *could have/ might have/must have/can't have*	94	Grammar	Account of a mugging	
40	Gather Together in My Name	96	Reading		*Gather Together in My Name* by Maya Angelou
Check/Use your English/Progress test		98–101			
41	Errol, a police officer	102	Character presentation	A police officer talks about her work	Errol, a police officer
42	Reported speech (1): statements and questions	104	Grammar		
43	Closing strategies	106	Communication	Ending conversations	
44	Reported speech (2): verbs of reporting	108	Grammar	A broken arrangement	
45	The changing role of the police	110	Reading	News report about violent behaviour	Changing role of the police
46	Past perfect simple	111	Grammar	Account of an unfortunate incident	
47	Mysteries and thrillers	112	Topic		Agatha Christie disappears
48	Expressing regrets	114	Communication	Regrets about past decisions	
49	Third conditional *if* clauses	116	Grammar	Conversation about an unusual robbery	News item
50	A Judgement in Stone	118	Reading	Radio panel discussion	Extract from a novel
Check/Use your English/Progress test		120–123			
Vocabulary list		124–125			
Student B material		126–128			

Speaking	Writing	Vocabulary	Discussion
Comparing personal experience	Informal letter	Products	Products
	Description of a famous monument or landmark	Word field: types of building	Opinions of the USA
Conversation about a special social event	Useful social information		Polite behaviour Etiquette and table manners
	Descriptive paragraph using defining relative pronouns		
	National stereotypes	Adjective formation: suffixes -less and -ful	Attitudes to the British Attitudes to foreigners as portrayed in jokes
	Justifying a job choice	Word field: jewellery and parts of the body Pronunciation of words ending in -ough	Key aspects of a job
Putting your views across			Choosing the perfect job
Dialogue – a phone call; roleplay requests for information	Short newspaper article		
Dialogue at a garage	Paragraphs comparing everyday life with other countries		Communication services: TV and telephone equipment
		Synonyms	Dress codes at work Attitudes to women in the work place
	Formal letter of complaint about football hooliganism		Responsibility Football hooliganism
	Contrasting sentences with linking device however	Verb and adjective formation from nouns	Ethics and personal dilemmas
Dialogue between a student and mother Discussing a job application	Letter of application	Abbreviations and acronyms Expressions deriving from work	
Roleplay a formal telephone conversation	Formal letter of request	Word field: physical violence	
	Short biography of a famous writer		Unmarried mothers Racism and discrimination by age
		Word field and derivation: crimes and criminals	Public perceptions of the police
Reporting missing property to the police	Report of a missing briefcase		
Dialogues outside college and in a café	Wriring an informal letter		
Act out a conversation about a visit to a disco	Informal letter		
		Prepositions after verbs	Public order and the police TV violence and crime
	A report from notes		
	Short composition about a mystery thriller you have read	Word field: types of books	The qualities of good popular fiction
Conversation about a late arrival	Short story about a regret		Social and environmental change
A dialogue about parking			What would you have done in certain situations?
	Punctuation; continuation of story	Adverb formation (ways of speaking); second syllable stress in adverbs	Coping with disabilities: illiteracy and dyslexia

Rapid review

PRESENT SIMPLE

1 Study the sentences and complete the rules.

I go to college in Valencia.
They have music lessons twice a week.
Do you like Mozart?
He doesn't like British cars.

1 The present simple is used to talk about events that are:
   a) always or nearly always true.
   b) happening now.
2 It is also used to talk about:
   a) things that you do frequently.
   b) things that you plan to do.

2 Write questions and short answers based on the pictures.

1 chips

4 dogs

'Does he like chips?'
'Yes, he does.'

2 fish

5 studying

3 opera

6 Kevin Costner

3 Complete the sentences with the correct form of the verbs in brackets.

1 What ... the word 'dull' ... ? (mean)
2 It ... 'not very interesting'. (mean)
3 How ... you ... your name? (spell)
4 My grandmother ... ... very well, does she? (not look)
5 I ... ... why you're wearing your coat indoors. (not understand)
6 ... you ... the first time we met? (remember)
7 She usually ... her parents every day. (phone)
8 The banks ... ... on Saturdays here. (not open)

ADVERBS AND ADVERBIAL PHRASES OF FREQUENCY

1 Study the sentences and complete the rules.

She usually wakes up at 6.30 every morning.
He's always late.
I've never eaten paella.
I see my grandmother once a month.

1 Adverbs like *usually*, *sometimes* and *never* come
   a) before
   b) after   the main verb in a sentence.
2 If there is an auxiliary verb (e.g. *has*, *is*) as well as a main verb, the adverb of frequency goes:
   a) before the auxiliary.
   b) in between the auxiliary and the main verb.
   c) after the main verb.
3 If the verb *to be* is the main verb, the adverb of frequency goes:
   a) before the verb *to be*.
   b) after the verb *to be*.
4 Adverbial phrases of frequency usually go:
   a) at the end of a sentence.
   b) in the same place as adverbs of frequency.

2 Rearrange the adverbs in order of frequency, starting with the most frequent.

sometimes   often   always   never   usually

3 Put the adverb or adverbial phrase in the correct place in the sentences.

1 I go to bed before midnight. (never)
2 She's had lunch by this time. (usually)
3 Do you go to discos? (ever)
4 I go to the dentist. (once a year)
5 She sees her boyfriend. (sometimes/six days a week)
6 He is very rude to people. (often)
7 I've liked him. (always)
8 We go to the cinema. (about twice a month)

4 Make a list of as many things as possible that you do: every day; once a week; once a month; once a year.

EXAMPLE
I have a bath every day. I go swimming once a week.

Read your list to your partner. What things do you have in common? What does your partner do that is different from you? Tell the class.

EXAMPLE
'We both get up at seven o'clock every day. Thomas runs round the park every morning but I don't.'

PRESENT CONTINUOUS

1 Study the sentences and complete the rules by choosing the correct letter(s).

Don't disturb him. He's writing a letter.
They're living in Greece at the moment.
I'm leaving on Friday.

1 The present continuous tense can be used to talk about:
  a) things which happen every day.
  b) things taking place at the time of speaking.
  c) current news.
  d) recent news.
  e) possible future plans.
  f) definite future arrangements.
2 The tense is formed by using the present tense of:
  a) *to have* b) *to be*
  followed by the main verb in the *-ing* form.

2 Look at the picture and correct the statements which Mrs Gibson makes about her family's routine.

'We lead a very quiet life in the evenings. My husband likes watching the nine o'clock news on television. I usually knit or sew in front of the TV. My son, Luke, does his homework and Suzy likes to read a book quietly. The dog usually sleeps beside the sofa and the cat sits by the window.'

1 Mr Gibson isn't watching television. He's sleeping.
2 Mrs Gibson ...   5 The dog ...
3 Luke ...   6 The cat ...
4 Suzy ...

3 Alison works in the tourist business. Look at the information about her travel arrangements for next week and answer the questions.

Alison Hale
Trip to the Czech Republic
15th April – 17th April

Wed: 15th April
London Heathrow BA765 Depart 16:30
Arrive Prague 19.45
Evening: Dinner with Mr Hlavka
  (Embassy representative)

Thurs: 16th April
Meet a representative from Prague
  Travel at 10 a.m.
Lunch with Mrs Hlavka
Afternoon: Free for sightseeing
Evening: Concert at Smetana Hall

Fri: 17th April
Morning: Attend conference at the
  Exhibition Hall
15.30 BA 766 Prague – London Heathrow

Write full sentences to describe:

1 her travel arrangements to and from Prague
2 her arrival time in Prague
3 what her arrangements are for Thursday morning
4 what her arrangements are for Thursday lunch
5 what her arrangements are for Thursday evening
6 what her arrangements are for Friday morning
EXAMPLE
1 She's leaving for Prague on Wednesday April 15th at 16.30 and returning on Friday April 17th at 15.30.

4 Complete the dialogue with the correct form of the present simple or present continuous.

Harry, a reporter, is interviewing Patsy James, a famous singer on her arrival from Los Angeles.

HARRY: Ms James – how long ... (1 you/stay) in Britain?
PATSY: I ... (2 spend) a week in London and a week in Manchester.
HARRY: Which ... (3 you/prefer), London or Manchester?
PATSY: I ... (4 not answer) that question. I ... (5 like) both cities.
HARRY: How many concerts ... (6 you/give)?
PATSY: Three in London and two in Manchester.
HARRY: ... (7 you/make) an album at the moment?
PATSY: Yes, I ... (8 usually/try) to record one new album a year. The present one ... (9 come along) very nicely.
HARRY: Great. I ... (10 hope) you have a very successful trip.
PATSY: Thank you.

GOING TO AND *WILL*

1 Study the sentences. Then write the number of the sentence which matches the correct use of *going to* or *shall/will* below.

1 *I'm going to see 'Philadelphia' this evening.*
2 *I'll have the chicken, please.*
3 *Don't worry. I'll send you a postcard.*
4 *Shall I give you some help with that?*
5 *She'll be twenty next week.*

a) making a prediction about a definite future event
b) offering help
c) talking about a future plan which you have already thought about
d) making a spontaneous decision
e) making a promise

2 Complete the sentences with *'ll, will* or *won't*.

1 That shopping looks heavy. I … carry some of it if you like.
2 I've never liked him. I … (not) be sorry when he's gone.
3 I can't believe it. My brother … be twenty-six next week.
4 She … phone as soon as she arrives in Sydney.
5 If I can find the book in the bookshop, I … buy you a copy.
6 Can you wait a moment? This … (not) take too long.
7 If you're having steak, I think I … have it too.
8 Don't throw that string away. My mother … use it for something, I'm sure.

3 Complete the dialogues with *going to* or *will*.

1 A: Why have you bought more eggs?
   B: I … make some mayonnaise. Oh no!
   A: What?
   B: I haven't got enough olive oil.
   A: I … go and get you some.

2 A: I'm just going out for a half an hour.
   B: … pass a newsagent?
   A: Maybe. I'm not sure. Why?
   B: It's O.K. I wanted the latest *Hello* magazine but I … get it tomorrow morning.

3 A: You're leaving early!
   B: I know. I … meet Tom for an early morning swim.
   A: That sounds fun. I think I … come too.

4 A: I can't bear it. You … leave in half an hour.
   B: Don't be sad. I … write to you every week. I promise.

PAST SIMPLE

1 Study the sentences and complete the rules.

I walked all the way into town yesterday.
The film started five minutes ago.
She arrived in Britain last week.

1 The past simple tense is used to talk about:
   a) a completed
   b) a continuing   event in the past.
2 A sentence in the past is often accompanied by a past time adverbial, e.g. *yesterday*, …, or …

2 Write the past simple form of these regular verbs.

walk   open   like   close   want   watch   hope   play
enjoy   ask   answer   try   die   happen   wait

3 Write the past simple form of these irregular verbs.

go   do   take   give   write   make   ring   know   find
leave   think   hear   say   get   sit

4 Complete the dialogue with the correct form of the past simple tense of the verbs in brackets.

ELAINE: You're very late! What time … (1 you/leave) home?
STEVE: Six o'clock. It … (2 take) me half an hour to get here.
ELAINE: … (3 you/come) by car?
STEVE: No, I … (4 catch) a bus. Anyway, let's go in. The concert starts in five minutes.
ELAINE: O.K. I hope you … (5 bring) the tickets.
STEVE: Don't worry. Oh no!
ELAINE: What?
STEVE: I … (6 change) jackets just before I … (7 leave) the house and I … (8 not realise) the tickets were still in my other jacket.
ELAINE: I don't believe it. You … (9 do) the same thing last time we … (10 go) to a concert!

PAST CONTINUOUS

1 Study the sentences and complete the rules.

What were you doing at nine o'clock last night?
She was working when I arrived.
I woke up feeling marvellous. The birds were singing and
the sun was shining.
Martin was working on a farm at the time.
I finished my book while the children were watching TV.

1 The past continuous tense almost always occurs after a
 clause introduced by the word:
 a) while.   b) when.
2 You use the past continuous to talk about:
 a) a completed past event.
 b) the background situation at a point of time in the
  past.
 c) something that was in progress at a specific time in
  the past.

2 Look at the pictures and say what was happening when Ann called at Sarah's house.

Ann called on a friend, Sarah, who is married with a family
of four children. It was six o'clock in the evening. It was
not a good time to call. When she arrived:
1 the baby was crying.   4 the telephone …
2 the children …   5 the supper …
3 the teenage daughter … 6 the dog …

3 Choose the correct verb form.

1 The old lady (crossed/was crossing) the road when the
 car hit her.
2 When I (woke up/was waking up), it (poured/was
 pouring) with rain.
3 What time (did you get up/were you getting up) today?
4 Who (did you talk to/were you talking to) when I rang?
5 While I (had/was having) breakfast, I (saw/was seeing)
 someone climb into my neighbour's garden.

PRESENT PERFECT SIMPLE

1 Study the sentences and complete the rules.

I've hurt my arm.
He's just finished school.
They've already had lunch.
I've written two letters so far today.
They've lived here since 1960.

1 The present perfect tense is used when referring to an
 action or event which:
 a) is happening now.   b) started in the past.
2 The action or event:
 a) is finished.   b) is still in progress.
 c) may or may not be still in progress.
3 If a speaker uses the present perfect tense to refer to
 an event in the past, he/she is:
 a) interested   b) not interested
 in the precise time when the event happened.

2 Complete the past participle forms of these irregular verbs.

do go be have bring take make read write
speak drive find break get buy lose

3 Which of the following adverbials would you use with the present perfect tense, and which with the past simple?

yet yesterday so far today just two minutes ago
in 1983 last week never already on Tuesday
ever since 1987

4 Use the verbs to ask questions with 'Have you ever …?'

EXAMPLE 1 Have you ever broken your leg?

1 break/leg   5 see/ghost
2 write/poem   6 be/Africa
3 sing/in public   7 drive/racing car
4 drink/champagne   8 stay up/all night

Ask questions with a partner. If the answer is *yes*, give details.

EXAMPLE 1 'Have you ever broken your leg?'
          'Yes, I have. I broke my leg last year.'

5 Complete the sentences with the present perfect or the past simple form of the verb in brackets.

1 I … (already/have) three cups of coffee this morning.
2 What time … (you/get) here?
3 … (you/eat) any lunch yet?
4 When … (he/arrive) in Istanbul?
5 … (you/ever/taste) Brazilian coffee?
6 You obviously enjoy your job. How long … (you/work)
 here?
7 I … (go) to the cinema on Saturday night.
8 What's the matter. You look as if you … (see) a ghost.

MODALS: *MUST, MUSTN'T, NEEDN'T, HAVE TO*

1 Match the sentences below with the correct description a)–e).

1 I'm tired. I must go to bed.
2 You must phone home before you leave.
3 You mustn't take more than two tablets.
4 You needn't go to the concert if you don't want to.
5 I have to be at work by eight o'clock tomorrow.

a) an obligation or strong recommendation from another speaker.
b) a duty or rule which comes from an outside authority.
c) a removal of an obligation to do something.
d) a personal decision which you feel strongly about.
e) something which you are not allowed to do or strongly advised not to do.

2 Complete the sentences with *must, mustn't* or *needn't*.

> **EXAMINATION RULES**
>
> Please take note!
>
> ❑ You … arrive five minutes before the exam starts.
> ❑ You … wear school uniform if you don't want to.
> ❑ You … talk once the exam starts.
> ❑ You … use a pen not a pencil to write your essays.
> ❑ You … stay for the three hours if you finish early.

3 Complete the paragraph about a lifeguard's job with the following forms of *have to.*

have to   had to   don't have to   didn't have to   will have to

'It's quite easy to get a job as a lifeguard. You …(1)… have any qualifications apart from a lifesaving certificate but of course you …(2)… be able to swim strongly. And there are lots of jobs around. I …(3)… search very hard to get this one. The job can be quite boring I suppose. Nothing much happens most days, but last week I …(4)… dive in and rescue a little boy who was in difficulties in the deep end. It's not terribly well paid. I think if they want us to stay, they …(5)… pay us a bit more.'

4 Think of rules and instructions for these situations, using *must, have to* and *mustn't*.

– crossing a busy road
– driving on a motorway
– on an aeroplane which is about to take off or land
– watching the lions in their cage at a zoo
– visiting someone in hospital
– waiting for the music to begin at a concert
– in a small rowing boat at sea

VERBS FOLLOWED BY *TO…* OR *…ING*

1 Study the sentences and put the verbs in italics in the correct column in your notebooks.

Verb + infinitive with *to*	Verb + *-ing* (gerund)

1 I *want* to go swimming this afternoon.
2 Do you *enjoy* meeting new people?
3 I *like* going by car when I'm in a hurry, but I *prefer* travelling by train when I've got a good book to read.
4 He *loves* playing with the children.
5 You *need* to eat some more fresh fruit.
6 Don't *try* to do too much in one day.
7 Have you *finished* reading the paper yet?
8 I *don't mind* waking up early but I *hate* getting out of bed.
9 You should *avoid* driving when you're feeling stressed.
10 What have you *decided* to do about your bike?

2 Match the sentence openers 1–8 with a suitable ending from the list a)–h) below.

1 I'm tired of staying at home every holiday. Next year I want …
2 I like parties because I enjoy …
3 I hate most housework but I don't mind …
4 I'm worried about my exams so I've decided …
5 I'm exhausted. I need …
6 Can I have that magazine after you've finished …
7 If you want to go out tonight, you must try …
8 If you're worried about your weight, you ought to avoid …

a) to get some sleep.
b) meeting new people.
c) reading it?
d) to finish some of your homework now.
e) doing the vacuum cleaning.
f) eating too much fatty food.
g) to do something really different.
h) to enrol on an intensive revision course.

3 Complete these sentences in any way you like.

1 When it's really cold and nasty outside, I love …
2 When I'm going on a long journey, I prefer …
3 I'm getting rather tired. I need …
4 Let's try and get there in good time. I hate …
5 Can we stop at the flower shop? I want …

ARTICLES, COUNTABLE AND UNCOUNTABLE NOUNS

1 Match the sentences 1–10 below with the correct description a)–j).

1 *He bought an apple. The apple was bad.*
2 *We had lunch at twelve o'clock.*
3 *She went to university in France.*
4 *I like coffee but not tea.*
5 *I'm travelling round the USA next summer.*
6 *She's a dentist.*
7 *We went by car.*
8 *The sun rises in the east.*
9 *He speaks Spanish well.*
10 *I'm not allowed to eat biscuits.*

You use the indefinite article *a* or *an*:
a) with jobs.
b) when you mention something for the first time.

You use the definite article *the*:
c) when you mention something for the second time.
d) when there is only one of something.
e) with certain countries and places.

You use no article:
f) with names of meals.
g) with certain public buildings or institutions.
h) with uncountable and plural nouns when used in a general sense.
i) before methods of transport used in a general sense.
j) with languages.

2 Complete the sentences by inserting *a*, *an*, *the* or '–' if no article is required.

ANN: Would you like ...(1)... sandwich?
JACK: No, I had ...(2)... lunch before I left ...(3)... home.
ANN: Well, ...(4)... sandwich I'm eating is disgusting. Do you like ...(5)... tuna fish?
JACK: No, I don't.
ANN: Here. Have ...(6)... orange.
JACK: I don't like ...(7)... oranges.
ANN: Are you serious? By the way, we have to see ...(8)... Principal at two o'clock.
JACK: Why?
ANN: He's holding ...(9)... meeting for all students who are going on to ...(10)... university.
JACK: Where's ...(11)... meeting?
ANN: It's in ...(12)... main hall. Come on, let's go.

3 Write the plurals of these countable nouns.

dog road country man woman child house
church person chicken fish

4 Arrange the following words into three columns corresponding to those words which can be preceded by *a/an*, *some* or *the*.

a/an	*some*	*the* (but not *some*)
table	furniture	government

table apple furniture potatoes suitcase
government bag luggage sugar police butter
chair people moon water news church
information kitchen Alps Pope weather advice

5 Complete the sentences with *some*, *any*, *the* or *a/an*.

1 Can I have ... cup of coffee, please?
2 He gave me ... useful information.
3 Have you got ... tea?
4 My mother has given me ... furniture for my flat.
5 This is serious. I think we should call ... police.
6 ... weather is getting worse.
7 They went for ... skiing holiday in ... Alps.
8 'Have you got ... luggage?' 'I've got ... suitcase and ... small shoulder bag.'

6 Correct the sentences.

1 His brother is architect.
2 I have the breakfast at seven o'clock.
3 After leaving the school, she went to Uppsala University
4 Have you finished book you bought last week?
5 Can you see Rocky Mountains from the plane?
6 The informations they gave me was wrong.

EXPRESSIONS OF QUANTITY: *MUCH, MANY, A FEW, A LITTLE, A LOT OF, PLENTY, TOO MUCH/MANY, NOT ENOUGH*

1 Study the sentences and complete the rules.

How much milk have we got?
How many people are there?
Are there many Spanish people there?
There are a few problems.
We've got a little time.
We've got plenty of time.
There are a lot of potatoes left.
Are there a lot of potatoes left?
He hasn't got much/a lot of experience.
We haven't got enough room.
There's too much meat.
There are too many questions and too little time.

1 *Many* and *much* are used in:
   a) positive statements.
   b) negative statements.
   c) questions.
2 *A lot of* is used in:
   a) positive statements.
   b) negative statements.
   c) questions.
3 *Many* and *a few* are used with:
   a) countable nouns.
   b) uncountable nouns.
4 *Much* and *a little* are used with:
   a) countable nouns.
   b) uncountable nouns.
5 With expressions using *not ... enough*, the word *enough* comes:
   a) before the noun.
   b) after the noun.

2 Write questions and answers using the prompts below.

EXAMPLE
A: How many tomatoes are there in the fridge?
B: There are plenty of tomatoes.

1 tomatoes/in the fridge: plenty
2 milk/in the jug: not much
3 people/in the room: a lot of
4 fruit/in the bowl: not enough
5 sport/on TV: too little
6 videos/on the shelf: not many
7 money/in the wallet: a lot of
8 eggs/in the box: a few

PREPOSITIONS OF TIME AND PLACE

1 Study the sentences and answer the questions.

He arrived in London on Monday.
She was born in Scotland in 1956.
The party is on June 8th at eight o'clock in the evening.
We usually go to the coast in summer.
My birthday is in May.
We checked-in at the airport at 6.30.
He drove to the station.
She arrived at Littlehampton by taxi.

Which preposition do you use:
a) with months, parts of the day, seasons, years?
b) with days of the week and dates?
c) with clock times?
d) with big cities and countries?
e) with places and small towns and villages?
f) to express motion towards somewhere?
g) with methods of transport?

2 Complete the sentences with the correct preposition from the following list. Some prepositions are used several times.

at   in   on   by   to   from

1 I was born ... 1975 ... Manchester.
2 I'll see you ... Tuesday.
3 I think I'll go ... train.
4 We're arriving ... June 4th ... 6.30 p.m.
5 You must arrive ... the airport an hour before the flight.
6 How long does it take you to get ... work from your house?
7 The shop is open ... nine ... the morning ... five o'clock ... the evening.
8 Our cat likes to go out ... night.
9 I like staying up late. I'm never ... bed before midnight.
10 I usually have lunch ... the canteen ... work.

3 Complete this paragraph about the famous author, Kingsley Amis' life.

Kingsley Amis was born ...(1)... South London ...(2)... 1922 and was educated ...(3)... the City of London school and ...(4)... St John's College, Oxford. ...(5)... 1949 ...(6)... 1963 he taught ...(7)... Swansea, Princeton and Cambridge University. His first novel *Lucky Jim* was published ...(8)... 1954.

COMPARISON OF ADJECTIVES

1 Complete the paradigms.

Adjective	Comparative	Superlative
clean	cleaner	cleanest
nice	…	…
big	bigger	…
dirty	dirtier	…
fat	…	…
happy	…	…
good	better	…
bad	worse	…
interesting	more interesting	… interesting
beautiful	… beautiful	most beautiful

2 Write two sentences for each statement.

EXAMPLE
1 The Amazon is longer than the Mississippi.
The Mississippi is shorter than the Amazon.

1 The Amazon is 6,300 km long; the Mississippi is 6,080 km long.

2 Mont Blanc is 4,814 metres high; the Matterhorn is 4,509 metres high.

3 A Ferrari can go at 255 kph; a Mercedes 380SL can go at 225 kph.

4 Gerry is 23 in August; Sue is still only 22.

5 The temperature in London today is 18°C; in Barcelona it's 25°C.

6 Peter is 180 cm tall whereas Tom is 175 cm.

7 The brown leather coat costs £120 but the black one costs £135.

8 My bag weighs 20 kilos; yours only weighs 18.

3 Write questions using the prompts below.

EXAMPLE
1 Which is the largest ocean in the world?

1 large/ocean/in the world
2 tall/building/in New York
3 expensive/car/in this showroom
4 good/restaurant/in this town
5 bad/time of year/to go to Britain
6 interesting/book/you have ever read
7 quick/way/to the station
8 hard/question/on the exam paper

4 Write sentences with *as … as* or *not as … as*.

EXAMPLE
1 Jan is not as old as Tanya.

1 Jan: age 18   Tanya: age 19
2 Leo Burrell: 100 metres – 9.85 secs
  Carl Lewis: 100 metres – 9.86 secs
3 George Harrison: fortune – £25 million
  Rod Stewart: fortune – £25 million
4 *Sister Act*: 2 hr 20 mins
  The Fugitive: 2 hr 35 mins
5 Lisbon: 25°C   Paris: 25°C
6 Kevin: IQ 120   Leonard: IQ 110
  (IQ = Intelligence Quotient: a way of measuring intelligence)

5 Helen spends a lot of her time travelling abroad in her job. Look at the chart which shows her opinions of Rome, Madrid and New York and complete the paragraph.

	Rome	Madrid	New York
beautiful	✗		
expensive		✗	
interesting to visit	✗		
dangerous			✗
lively		✗	
relaxed			✗

She thinks Rome is the most beautiful city as well as …(1)… because of the number of historical buildings. Madrid, on the other hand, is …(2)… but, in her opinion, it is …(3)… of the three cities. As for New York, she thinks it is definitely …(4)…, especially late at night, but of all the three she thinks it is …(5)…

–1–
Nick

A student

Nick Harrington is eighteen and in his final year at school. He's taking three 'A' levels this summer in Maths, Physics and Computer Studies. Unfortunately, he hasn't worked very hard and his teachers are not happy with his progress. They think he is spending too much time playing his guitar and reading music magazines.

'We're supposed to spend every evening and weekend revising for exams but I can't be bothered. I hate revising. It's so boring. I'll be glad to see the last of my physics textbook. I'm sorry I didn't take music instead for 'A' level.'

Although he claims that he can't sing very well, Nick is quite a talented musician and plays the piano as well as the guitar. 'One thing which impresses people is that I can listen to something and then just play it. I'm lucky, I suppose. I've got a good ear for music.'

In his spare time he plays in a band. They usually play together three evenings a week. He has given a few concerts at school but he's not allowed to give any public performances in town. He would like someone important in the music business to 'discover' him but he knows that is easier said than done.

Nick goes to an expensive private boarding school called Eton, where he lives during the term. His friends at home who go to the local state school sometimes tease him about going to a private school. Nick doesn't care too much about what they say. 'School's only a small part of your life. In some ways it doesn't really matter where you go. It's the future that's important. The best part of this year is that I'm leaving school at the end of term!'

Words to learn
revise   claim   talented   impress   tease

1 Read and answer.

1 What subjects is Nick taking for his 'A' levels?
2 Why are Nick's teachers not pleased with him?
3 What is Nick supposed to do every evening and weekend?
4 In what ways is Nick a talented musician?
5 Why do Nick's friends from home tease him?

2 Read and think.

1 How do you think Nick's parents feel about Nick's progress at school?
2 How do you think Nick spends most evenings and weekends?
3 Why is it going to be hard for him to be discovered?
4 Why do you think Nick's friends tease him about going to a private school?

3 About you

1 Do you think revising for exams is boring?
2 How much of your spare time do you spend listening to or playing music?
3 Is your school a private or a state school?
4 Are there many private schools in your country? What sort of people go to them?

VOCABULARY

1 What do you think these words and expressions from the text mean?

can't be bothered   to see the last of
have a good ear   to 'discover'
easier said than done

2 In pairs, discuss the difference in meaning between the following:

private/state school   day/boarding school
primary/secondary school
to go to college/to get into college
to take/pass/fail an exam
to get a pass/good grade/degree

3 ▭ Listen to how the following are stressed.

DAY school   STATE school   PRImary school
BOARDing school

Write the words below with the correct stress in capital letters. Then say them aloud.

night school   private school   public school
evening class   English class

▭ LISTENING

Before you listen

Look at the statements on the right. Which ones indicate that the speaker: a) approves of private schools; b) disapproves of private schools?

LISTEN

Three other people give their opinions of private schools. Listen and note whether the speaker approves or disapproves of these schools.

1 'I think all private education is unfair.'

2 'I'd like to go to a private school if I could be sure of getting better 'A' level grades there.'

3 'People who go to private schools think they are better than anyone else.'

4 'I don't think there is anything wrong with paying for your education.'

5 'I honestly think they have no idea how anyone lives in the real world.'

-2-

Grammar

Present simple and continuous

What's the difference in meaning?

1 Nick plays the guitar.
2 Nick is playing the guitar.

Which verb tense is used in each sentence? Look back at the text about Nick in Unit 1. Can you find some examples of these tenses? Check the Focus section below to see the different ways in which the two tenses are used.

FOCUS
The present simple

This tense is used

- to talk about general facts which are true most or all of the time:
  Nick goes to a private boarding school.

- to talk about routine and frequency:
  They usually play together three evenings a week.

- with verbs of emotion, e.g. *like, love, hate, want*:
  I hate revising.

- with verbs of thinking, e.g. *think, know, understand*:
  He knows that is easier said than done.

The present continuous

This tense is used

- to talk about events which are happening now or around the time of speaking:
  He is spending too much time playing his guitar.

- to talk about definite arrangements in the future:
  He's taking three 'A' levels this summer.

- When referring to the future, the tense occurs particularly with verbs like *go, come, see, visit, meet, arrive* and *leave*, which are often connected with timetables and diary arrangements:
  He's leaving on Friday.

Note
The present continuous is not generally used with verbs of emotion and thinking.

PRACTICE

1 Use the text about Nick in Unit 1 to write questions for these answers.

EXAMPLE
1 Eighteen.
   How old is Nick?

2 Maths, Physics and Computer Studies.
3 Because it's boring.
4 The piano and the guitar.
5 He plays in a small band.
6 Three evenings a week.
7 A private boarding school.
8 At the end of term.

2 Look at the chart on the right. Ask and answer about Nick, Beth and Tom. Use the present simple or present continuous tense.

EXAMPLES
A: Where does Nick live?
B: He lives with his parents near London.

A: Apart from 'A' levels, what else is he doing at the moment?
B: He's making a 'demo' tape.

3 Interview your partner and make a similar chart. After the interview, close your notebooks and tell the class as much as you can remember about your partner.

NICK

Home with parents near London
Favourite magazine New Musical Express
Favourite food steak and chips
Interests playing the guitar
Exams 'A' level Maths, Physics, Computer Studies
Current activity making a 'demo' tape
Ambition to be a musician

BETH

Home small village near Bath
Favourite magazine The Face
Favourite food pasta
Interests reading
Exams 'A' level English, History, Economics
Current activity learning to drive
Ambition to be a journalist

TOM

Home with parents in Reading
Favourite magazine The Biker
Favourite food Indian Food
Interests cycling
Exams 'A' level Portuguese, Spanish, English
Current activity training for the Round Britain Cycle Race
Ambition to be a travel courier

🖭 LISTENING

Listen to an announcement for a new TV soap opera about a theatre family called 'The Hartleys'.
Draw a family tree for the Hartley family and then write at least one fact about each person.

EXAMPLE
Charles is a famous actor.

WRITING

1 Before you write

Look at the picture below and read the paragraph about Nick's father.

Rex Harrington is Nick's father. He is a rich businessman of about forty-five. He's tall and dark. He wears dark suits but at weekends he wears casual clothes. He usually gets up at six, does some exercises and then goes to the office. He never gets back before ten o'clock at night so he doesn't see much of his family. He is interested in collecting pictures of horses. At the moment he is travelling on business in America because he's opening an office over there next year.

2 Use the text about Nick's father as a model to write about someone you know.

Say what they do and how old they are. Describe what they look like and what sort of clothes they wear. Describe part of their daily routine and what their interests are. Finish by describing their current activities, future plans and ambitions. Link your sentences with *and, but, then, so* and *because*. Include some time markers like *at the moment*.

3 Now write about yourself in the same way.

−3−

Communication

Shopping

Look at the photograph above and answer the questions.

1 What sort of shop is it?
2 What is the young woman buying?
3 How much does a CD or music cassette cost in your country?

🔊 DIALOGUE

WOMAN: Excuse me, have you got the latest Pink Floyd album on CD?
ASSISTANT: No, I'm afraid we've completely sold out.
WOMAN: Oh, pity. Do you have *Zooropa* by U2?
ASSISTANT: Yes, I think it's in stock. One moment and I'll check.
WOMAN: Thanks.
ASSISTANT: Yes, here we are.
WOMAN: Great. How much is it?
ASSISTANT: £13.99.
WOMAN: O.K. I'll have it.
ASSISTANT: Right. Here's your change and your receipt.
WOMAN: Thanks.

Listen and answer the questions.

1 Which CDs does the woman ask for?
2 Which of these does she buy?
3 How much is it?
4 Why couldn't she buy the other one?

PRACTICE

1 Act out conversations.

You have a list of things to buy in a stationery shop. The shop assistant has prices and details of what is available in the shop. Sometimes the item you want will not be available so you must decide whether to buy an alternative item or not. In pairs, practise several conversations changing parts.

CUSTOMER'S LIST	ASSISTANT'S NOTES
Tina Turner's Greatest Hits	*Tina Turner's Greatest Hits:* sold out
The Rats by James Herbert	All paperback books £4.99
Airmail writing paper	Writing paper: airmail £2.65
Coloured marker pens	Coloured marker pens 99p each. Only red and green.
	Magazines in stock:
	Vogue £2.70, *Arena* £2.20
Beat magazine	Sold out: *Hondo, Beat, Mizz*

Start like this:
CUSTOMER: Excuse me. Have you got *Tina Turner's Greatest Hits*?
ASSISTANT: No, I'm afraid we . . .

2 In pairs, use the dialogue and the pictures below to shop for clothes.

CUSTOMER: Excuse me, can I try this jacket on?
ASSISTANT: Yes, of course.
(a few minutes later)
Any good?

c: Yes, it's fine. How much is it?
A: It's £125.50.
c: Yes, I think I'll have it, please.
A: Fine, I'll put it in a bag.

c: No, I'm afraid it's not quite what I want. I think I'll leave it, thank you.
A: O.K.

LISTENING
Before you listen

1 Name as many different types of music as you can.
2 What else, apart from CDs and music cassettes, can you buy in a big music store?
3 What different ways can you pay for goods in a shop?

Listen to the conversation in a music shop.

Note down:
the two things the customer came to buy.
why she did not buy them.
what she finally bought.
what they cost and how she paid.

WRITING

Write a dialogue. You are in a music shop and you ask an assistant if she's got a particular CD or cassette. She says she hasn't and gives a reason. You then ask about another CD. When she brings it, ask how much it costs. Decide if you are or are not going to buy it.

£44.99 £125.50 £64.95 £69.99 £24.99

Grammar

Not allowed to and not supposed to

📼 DIALOGUE

One Saturday afternoon, Nick passes a crowd of people outside the Theatre Royal, Windsor.

NICK: Hello, Alex.
ALEX: Oh, hi Nick!
NICK: What's happening?
ALEX: We're waiting to see Timothy Dalton. I want to get his autograph.
NICK: Why don't you go in?
ALEX: We're not allowed to. We have to wait until he comes out.
MAN: Come on, you lot, move on. You know you're not supposed to block the street.
ALEX: Here he is!

Later
ALEX: Well at least I got his autograph! Do you want to come and have a coffee?
NICK: O.K. but it'll have to be quick. I'm supposed to be revising.

Listen and answer the questions.

1 Why are the girls waiting outside the theatre?
2 Why can't they go in?
3 Why is the doorman irritated?
4 What does Alex invite Nick to do?
5 Why does Nick say: 'It'll have to be quick'?

FOCUS

'Not allowed to'
● This is used when the speaker is giving a definite rule:
We're not allowed to go in the theatre.

'Not supposed to'
● This is often used when talking about a rule which people sometimes break.
You're not supposed to block the street.

Note
In the positive: *allowed to* = have permission to, but *supposed to* = have an obligation to i.e. it is expected behaviour.

Look back at the text about Nick in Unit 1 and find examples of *(not) allowed to* and *(not) supposed to*.

PRACTICE

1 Write restrictions and rules for the following places or situations.

EXAMPLE
1 In an aeroplane you're not allowed to smoke in the toilets. You're not supposed to stand up until the plane comes to a complete halt.

1 in an aeroplane
2 in a petrol station
3 on a motorway
4 in a library
5 visiting people in hospital
6 in your school

2 Look at the signs below and state the rules connected with them using *not allowed to* and *not supposed to*.

No right turn

Don't drop litter! £20 fine

Thank you for not smoking in this office.

It is illegal to travel without a ticket.

Please keep our city clean. Don't drop litter.

No parking between 08.00 and 18.30.

Please do not talk to the driver.

3 📼 Listen to this announcement.

Note down:
where the announcement is taking place.
what two things are not allowed.

Reading

Before you read

1 Do you have any brothers or sisters? Did your parents bring you up differently from them? In what ways?
2 What sort of toys did you have as a child?
3 Can you remember any bullies at your school?
4 What do you think of men who cry?

Guess the meaning

under pressure   stand up for himself   suffer
tease   bully   conformist   rebel   reduce

COMPREHENSION

Read the article on the right and answer the questions.

1 How do parents often distinguish between baby boys and baby girls?
2 In what ways are boys supposed to be 'macho'?
3 What often happens to boys who are not macho?
4 How can we reduce bullying?

THINK ABOUT IT

1 What are girls supposed to be good at?
2 How does this influence the way girls plan their future?

WRITING

Linking devices: *both . . . and, as well as, neither . . . nor*

*She likes **both** watching football **and** playing it.*
*She likes watching football **as well as** playing it.*
*Football is **neither** fun to play **nor** very exciting to watch.*

Write sentences of your own, using each of the linking devices above.

VOCABULARY

'macho' is the opposite of *'wimp'*, and *rebel* is the opposite of *conformist*.

Use a dictionary to find the opposites of:

big   brave   extrovert   hard
hardworking   noisy   strong   tall

UNDERSTANDING BOYS

BOYS AS BABIES

The education of children starts as soon as they are born; girls wear pink and boys wear blue; boys play with guns and girls play with dolls. Boys are allowed to make more noise and cause more trouble, while girls are supposed to be more interested in talking to and understanding people. This kind of education prepares boys for power in the world but for little else.

BOYS UNDER PRESSURE

A boy is under pressure in many ways. He is supposed to be 'macho' – good at sport, able to stand up for himself in fights and to suffer pain without crying. If he can't, he is a 'wimp' and often other boys will tease and bully him, especially at school. Yet probably only a very few boys can do all of these things. All boys are different – they have different needs and talents, likes and dislikes. Some boys are good at cooking and writing poetry whereas others are good at football or maths.

Boys aren't just 'machos' and 'wimps'; there are swots as well as sports stars, conformists as well as rebels, shy boys as well as girl-chasers. If we can assure them that all these types are okay, it may help to reduce the bullying of those boys who are the least macho.

> **Glossary**
> **'machos'** and **'wimps'** tough people and weak people, usually applied to men or boys
> **swot** a person who studies hard all the time

-6-
Grammar

Past simple and continuous

One evening last year Sue drove into a garage to get some petrol.
While she was paying for the petrol, a boy stole her wallet from the car.

Which tense is used in the first sentence above and which tenses in the second sentence?
Look at the Focus section below and notice how the tenses are used.

FOCUS

The past simple

This tense is used
- to talk about complete actions or events in the past. The tense is often linked to a time expression like *yesterday, last summer, in 1980*:
  One evening last year Sue drove into a garage to get some petrol.

The past continuous

This tense is used
- to talk about an activity which someone was in the middle of doing at a certain time in the past:
  What were you doing at six o'clock last night?
  I was watching the news on television.

- to talk about interrupted events in the past:
  While/When/she was paying for the petrol, a boy stole her wallet from her car.
  The position of *when* can be changed to give dramatic emphasis:
  She was paying for her petrol when suddenly a boy knocked her over and took her wallet.

- to describe background detail when telling a story:
  It was a warm summer's day. The sun was shining and the birds were singing.

What's the difference in meaning?

1 When she woke up, the telephone rang.
2 When she woke up, the telephone was ringing.

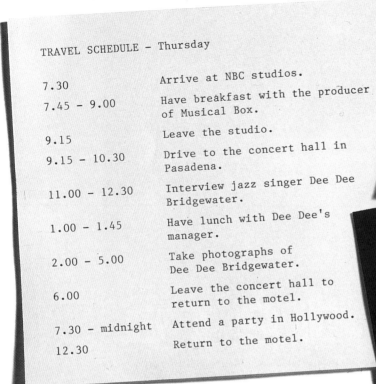

```
TRAVEL SCHEDULE - Thursday

7.30                    Arrive at NBC studios.

7.45 - 9.00             Have breakfast with the producer
                        of Musical Box.

9.15                    Leave the studio.

9.15 - 10.30            Drive to the concert hall in
                        Pasadena.

11.00 - 12.30           Interview jazz singer Dee Dee
                        Bridgewater.

1.00 - 1.45             Have lunch with Dee Dee's
                        manager.

2.00 - 5.00             Take photographs of
                        Dee Dee Bridgewater.

6.00                    Leave the concert hall to
                        return to the motel.

7.30 - midnight         Attend a party in Hollywood.

12.30                   Return to the motel.
```

PRACTICE

1 Sue Barnes is a young Scottish music journalist on her first visit to California. Look at the travel notes above for the last day of her visit. In pairs, ask and say what Sue did: 1 before lunch, 2 after lunch, 3 in the evening.

EXAMPLE
A: What did Sue do before lunch?
B: First she arrived and had breakfast at NBC studios. Then she...

2 In pairs, ask and say what Sue was doing at the following times:

1 8.00	3 12.00	5 3.00 p.m.
2 10.00	4 1.30 p.m.	6 9.00 p.m.

EXAMPLE
1 A: What was Sue doing at eight o'clock?
  B: She was having breakfast at NBC studios.

3 Write the correct form of the verbs in brackets to complete and continue Sue's story. Use the past simple or the past continuous tense.

While Sue Barnes, a reporter for the New Musical Express, (travel) round the USA last year, she (have) an unpleasant experience. She had interviewed a jazz singer and had recorded the interview on a cassette which (be) on the front seat of her car together with other personal belongings.

She (drive) back to her motel after a party in Hollywood on her last night when she (realise) that she (run out) of petrol. She (stop) at an all-night garage just off the main highway. She (fill) the petrol tank, (take) 20 dollars from her wallet and (go) to the kiosk to pay. While she (pay), a boy suddenly (appear) from the shadows, (open) her car door and (take) her wallet, passport and return air ticket – and her cassette!

 LISTENING

Listen to a friend of Sue's retelling the story at a party and note the details which he gets wrong.

WRITING

Write an account of an incident which has happened to you or someone you know. Say when and where the incident took place, who was involved and what they were doing at the time. Describe what happened, adding background details where necessary.

EXAMPLE
Last Saturday night I went with some friends to see the new Eddy Murphy film. We were queuing outside the cinema when suddenly a man came up . . .

Banderas
International filmstar

Already immensely popular in his native Spain, Antonio Banderas has recently leapt to international stardom with important roles in three major Hollywood films in quick succession.

In *Philadelphia*, the first major Hollywood film about an AIDS victim, he starred with Oscar-winning Tom Hanks. Then, in the film of Isabel Allende's novel, *The House of the Spirits*, he co-starred with Meryl Streep and Jeremy Irons. In *Interview with a Vampire*, he played opposite Tom Cruise and Brad Pitt. However, he is probably more famous as the man who said 'No' to Madonna when he told her that he was married.

'I was born in Málaga in 1960. I finished elementary school at the age of thirteen and went to Málaga's School of Dramatic Art until I was eighteen. It was tough but exciting. We had a truck and we travelled throughout Spain with our plays. Everyone did everything – scenery, costumes, make-up. It was great training.

After graduating I went to Madrid. I did some TV work and got a job in a small theatre. A year later, after a matinée performance one day, someone said: "There's a young director outside who wants to meet you."

Then this man opened my dressing room door and said "Do you want to make a movie with me?" And I said "Yeah!" The director was Pedro Almodóvar. During the eighties we worked together closely and for the next nine years I had some great parts in Pedro's films. Eventually I went to Hollywood to make *The Mambo Kings* in 1992. It was a sensible decision for my career but hopefully I'll work with Pedro again in the future.

When I got the part in *The Mambo Kings*, I knew only a few words of English. I had to spend eight hours a day learning English. Now I even dream in English.

I am married to actress, Ana Leza. I don't really live a glamorous life, not like people imagine a filmstar lives. We have a comfortable apartment in the centre of Madrid. I play tennis. I play the piano. I go to bed fairly early. I also want to raise a family.

Nowadays, with all my Hollywood filming, I don't spend as much time as I would like in Spain. I have to spend a lot of time in America. I prefer New York to Los Angeles because it's real. When people get angry they show it. In L.A. people say everything is wonderful but it's not. But whatever happens, Spain will always be my home. I don't want to lose my roots. I think a man without roots is a nobody.'

–7–

Topic

A career in films

Before you read

Look at the photograph and discuss the questions in pairs.

1 Have you seen any films with Antonio Banderas in them?
2 Why do you think he is popular?
3 What difficulties do you think he has had to become an international filmstar?
4 Make a list of words you know to do with films and film production.

Words to learn

immensely   leap   in quick succession   victim
tough   truck   costumes   sensible   glamorous
raise   roots

1 Read and find out:

Why are the following important in Antonio Banderas' life?

1 Málaga's School of Dramatic Art
2 Pedro Almodóvar
3 *The Mambo Kings*
4 Tom Hanks
5 Madonna

2 Write questions.

Write at least six questions which the interviewer asked Antonio Banderas. Use the following question words: *When? Where? How? What? Why? How long?*

3 Read and think.

1 How do you think Almodóvar felt when Banderas went to Hollywood to make *The Mambo Kings*?
2 What do people expect the life of a famous star to be like?
3 What does he feel people from Los Angeles are like?

VOCABULARY

1 Complete the list of adverbs below.

ADJECTIVE	ADVERB	ADJECTIVE	ADVERB
sensible	sensibly	hopeful	...
dreadful	...	wonderful	...
beautiful	...	helpful	...
awful	...	terrible	...

2 🔲 Listen and note where the main stress falls on the adjective and adverb.

3 Which of the adjectives in Exercise 1 can follow *very*?

EXAMPLE: She is very sensible.

4 Which of the adverbs in Exercise 1 can be used instead of *very*?

EXAMPLE: It is dreadfully hot.

🔲 LISTENING

Listen to someone talking about an amusing incident. Note down the key points. Then listen again and note down any words or phrases about time. Use your notes to retell the story.

WRITING

Read the facts below about Antonio Banderas, then write them in chronological order. Notice how the time connectors in italics link the facts.

1 *After graduating* from the School of Dramatic Art, he got a small job in a theatre.
2 *Eventually* he went to Hollywood to make 'The Mambo Kings' and his international career started from there.
3 *A year later,* he met the Spanish director, Pedro Almodóvar.
4 He was born in Málaga *in 1960*.
5 He and Pedro worked together closely *during the eighties* and *for the next nine years* he had some great parts in Pedro's films.
6 He finished elementary school *at the age of 13* and went to Málaga's School of Dramatic Art *until he was 18*.

Now make notes about your own life or the life of someone in your family. Link these notes into a written paragraph using time connectors like those above.

$-8-$

Communication

Apologies

List as many ways of apologising as you can and then look at the picture and answer the questions.

1 Do you think the man in the picture is angry?
2 What is the girl saying?

▣ DIALOGUE

FATHER: What sort of time do you call this?
GIRL: I'm sorry.
FATHER: So you should be! It's two a.m!
GIRL: Oh Dad, do stop nagging. I'm over seventeen. It's up to me what time I come in.
FATHER: Not while you're living here, it isn't. Anyway, what on earth were you doing until two in the morning?
GIRL: We weren't doing anything. We were just talking.
FATHER: I was worried stiff about you.
GIRL: Honestly, Dad, I really am sorry, but you don't have to wait up for me, you know.
FATHER: O.K. I know you think I'm fussing and I'm sorry, but next time just let me know if you're going to be late, O.K? Give me a ring or something.
GIRL: Yes, O.K. I'll let you know next time. Sorry, Dad.
FATHER: That's O.K.

1 Listen and answer the questions.

1 Why is the girl's father angry?
2 What does the girl's father want her to do in future?
3 How often does the girl apologise? What does she say each time?
4 What three expressions does the father use in response to her apologies?

2 What do you understand by these idiomatic expressions?

1 What sort of a time do you call this?
2 So you should be.
3 It's up to me.
4 worried stiff
5 let me know
6 Give me a ring.

FOCUS

Apologies and responses

- Apologising:
  Sorry.
  I'm sorry.
  I'm terribly sorry.
  I'm awfully sorry.
  I really am sorry.

- Responding to apologies:
  That's O.K.
  That's all right.
  Don't worry about it.
  Never mind. It's nothing to worry about.
  It doesn't matter.

PRACTICE

1 Match the pictures 1 to 5 on the right with a suitable explanation from the list (a) to (e) below.

EXAMPLE
Picture 1 - b

a) There was a strike on the underground.
b) I wasn't looking where I was going.
c) I didn't realise it was so late.
d) I was only putting them back in the cupboard.
e) I thought it was mine.

Now, in pairs, act out each scene with an apology and explanation.

EXAMPLE
1 A: I'm sorry. I wasn't looking where I was going.
   B: That's O.K. There isn't much room in here.

2 In pairs, put the following situations in order from the least annoying to the most annoying.

1 A friend borrows your flippers to use on holiday and leaves them in the resort hotel.
2 A friend forgets to buy you some bread which you need for a party.
3 It is 3 a.m. The phone rings and it's a wrong number.
4 A friend spills black coffee over your new white jacket.

Now act out three of the situations in pairs.

EXAMPLE
A: I'm terribly sorry. I'm afraid I left your flippers in Ibiza.
B: Never mind. I can buy another pair.
A: Oh no, I'll get another pair for you.

🔊 LISTENING

Listen to an incident at a party and note:
1 what the woman did by accident.
2 how she apologised.
3 what the host said.
4 how the woman offered to make amends.
5 if her host accepted the offer.

Can you remember an incident when you had to apologise?

WRITING

Look at your notes from the Listening exercise and write the letter that the woman wrote to her host, Robert.
In your letter:
Thank Robert for the party and say how much you enjoyed it.
Apologise again for breaking the vase.
Make amends by asking if you can replace it.
Thank him again and say you hope to see him soon.

The following phrases may be useful:
I'm so sorry I . . . (past tense)
I'm terribly sorry about . . . -ing
I do apologise for . . . -ing
I'd like to . . .
I hope you'll let me . . .

I'M SO SORRY...

Grammar

Used to and be used to

Sue says: 'I grew up on a farm, so we always had masses of meat and dairy products. We used to eat red meat nearly every day of the week, and we used to have butter and cream with everything. But a few years ago I became much more conscious of my diet. I don't eat red meat at all now, and very little butter or cream. I'm used to eating salads and vegetables instead, in fact I'm used to a much lighter diet.'

What's the difference in meaning?

1 I used to eat red meat.
2 I'm used to eating red meat.

FOCUS

'Used to' (past habit)

* *Used to* followed by an infinitive is always a past tense. It does not have a present form. The tense is used to show that something which regularly happened in the past, i.e. a past habit, no longer occurs now.
  (Past)   *Years ago I used to eat a lot of red meat.*
  (Present) *I don't eat red meat at all now.*

'Be used to' (present custom)

* *To be used to* means *to be accustomed to* something. It can be followed by an *ing* form of the verb, or by a noun:
  I'm used to eating salads.
  I'm used to a lighter diet.

Find examples of the structures *used to* and *be used to* in the text about Sue at the top of the page.

PRACTICE

1 Match the sentences about Sue. Join the sentences with *but* and make statements about her life as a child compared with her life now, using *used to*.

EXAMPLE
Sue used to eat a lot of meat but now she is mainly vegetarian.

PAST HABITS
1 ate a lot of meat
2 had milk and cream with everything
3 went on holiday with her family
4 lived on a farm
5 drove a Fiat Uno

PRESENT HABITS
goes on holiday with friends
lives in a flat in Manchester
cycles everywhere
is mainly vegetarian
drinks tea and coffee without milk

2 Tell your partner about changes in your life concerning daily routine, family occasions, education and work using *used to*.

EXAMPLE
I used to eat a big breakfast before going to work, but I don't now.

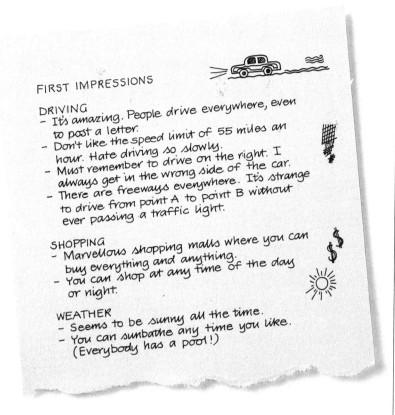

FIRST IMPRESSIONS

DRIVING
- It's amazing. People drive everywhere, even to post a letter.
- Don't like the speed limit of 55 miles an hour. Hate driving so slowly.
- Must remember to drive on the right. I always get in the wrong side of the car.
- There are freeways everywhere. It's strange to drive from point A to point B without ever passing a traffic light.

SHOPPING
- Marvellous shopping malls where you can buy everything and anything.
- You can shop at any time of the day or night.

WEATHER
- Seems to be sunny all the time.
- You can sunbathe any time you like. (Everybody has a pool!)

3 At the moment Sue has an assignment in California. She finds the lifestyle there very different from Britain. Imagine you are Sue. Use her notes above to say what you aren't used to in California.

EXAMPLE
I'm not used to driving everywhere.

4 Sue's brother, David, is in his first term at university. Read his account of being a student.

'At the moment it's a bit hard because I'm not used to living away from home. I have to do everything for myself, like cooking, washing and ironing. Mum used to do all that! Studying here is very different from school. We have to choose which lectures to go to and plan our own timetable. At school they used to tell you what to do and when to do it, but here you have more freedom. I'm not used to that so I often leave my essays to the last minute. Then I have to work right through the night, which is something I've never done before.'

5 Write as many sentences as you can about the things David is not used to doing.

EXAMPLE
He's not used to living away from home.

ACT IT OUT

In pairs, act out a conversation between Sue and a friend about how her brother is settling down at university.

Start like this:

FRIEND: How's your brother settling down at university?

SUE: O.K. but it's a bit hard for him because he's not used to living away from home.

🔲 LISTENING

Before you listen

Imagine you are spending some time in Britain. In groups, make a list of some of the features of the British way of life which you might find difficult or unusual. Here are some notes to start your list:
– speaking English all the time
– the noise and the traffic in London
– the unreliable English weather
– English money
– English food

Listen
Some young foreign students are studying in Britain. What features of British life aren't they used to? Are they the same as the ones you discussed?

WRITING

Imagine you are the last student in the Listening exercise. Write one paragraph of a letter to a penfriend describing the three aspects of British life which you are not used to. Link your sentences with:
Another thing is, . . . and
Also, . . .

EXAMPLE
When I first arrived, I wasn't used to the noise of the traffic and I couldn't sleep for three days, but it's all right now. Another thing was/is . . .

29

Reading

Cider with Rosie is a modern classic by Laurie Lee. It describes the time when he was growing up just after the First World War. Lee was one of a family of eight who lived in a cottage in the Cotswolds in what was then a remote part of the English countryside. The world which Laurie Lee describes has now vanished.

⋙ CIDER WITH ROSIE ⋘

With our mother, then, there were eight of us in that cottage, using rooms on its three large floors. There was the very big white attic where the girls used to sleep. On the floor below, Mother and Tony shared one bedroom; Jack, Harold and I had the other. But the house had been so often changed, since its building, that it was almost impossible to get to one's room without first passing through someone else's. So each night there was a procession of half-seen figures going sleepily to bed, until the last candle was blown out.

But most of the time when we were awake, while we were growing up, we spent in the kitchen. Until we married or ran away, it was the common room we all shared. In it, we lived and ate in the thick air of crowded family life; we didn't mind the little space; we trod on each other like birds in a nest, pushed past each other without unfriendliness, all talking at the same time or all silent. But we never, think, felt overcrowded, because we were as separate a the notes of a piano.

That kitchen, showing the marks of our boots and ou lives, was untidy, warm and low. Its muddle of furnitur seemed never the same; it was moved around every day Coal and sticks of beech wood crackled in a black fireplac and stove; towels hung to dry on the fireguard; the mante piece above the stove held an untidy collection of fine ol china and potatoes of unusual shape. On the floor ther were strips of muddy matting; the windows were crowde with plants in pots; the walls supported stopped clock and picture postcards. There were six tables of differen sizes; some armchairs with thei insides bursting out; boxes, book and papers on every chair; a so for cats, a small organ for coats and a piano for dust an photographs. And on th floor all round everythin the years had made shape less piles of Mother's new papers.

> **Glossary**
> **the Cotswolds** a hilly area in the west of England famous for its picturesque countryside and villages
> **beech** a tall tree with dark green or copper-coloured leaves
> **organ** a musical instrument, made of many pipes, played like a piano and often found in churches

Before you read

1 Look at the illustration. What details make the house seem old-fashioned?
2 Write down as many words as you can which are connected with rooms, furniture and fittings.

Guess the meaning

attic   share   procession
candle   trod (tread)   crackle
mantelpiece   matting
bursting out   shapeless piles

COMPREHENSION

1 Answer the questions.

1 How many people lived in the cottage?
2 Where did the family spend most of their time?
3 What musical instruments were there in the kitchen?

2 Correct the statements.

EXAMPLE
1 Laurie Lee grew up in a small cottage.
No, Laurie Lee grew up in a large cottage.

2 The girls slept in separate rooms.
3 The kitchen had a very high ceiling.
4 The kitchen had a fitted carpet.
5 There were six tables of the same size.
6 All the books were in a bookcase.
7 The newspapers were all in very neat piles.

THINK ABOUT IT

1 Do you think Laurie Lee came from a wealthy family?
2 Why do you think some of the family ran away?
3 What do you think Laurie Lee's mother was like?

ABOUT YOU

1 How big is your family?
2 What interesting things do your remember from your childhood?
3 Do any of your older relatives have interesting memories of how life used to be?

STYLE

1 Look at these similes from the text. They describe one thing by comparing it with another.

as separate as the notes of a piano   like birds in a nest

Complete the similes below.

as white as . . .   as strong as . . .   as tall as . . .
She/He sang like . . .   She/He swam like . . .   She/He ran like . . .

2 What do the following phrases tell you about life in the cottage?

a sofa for cats   a piano for dust   an organ for coats

TALKING POINT

What are the advantages and disadvantages of growing up in a large family?

VOCABULARY

Look at the following nouns from the text:

fireplace   fireguard

Link a word from the top line with a word from the bottom line to form a compound noun.

arm   house   table   candle   window   wash   book   dining
sill   basin   case   chair   work   room   cloth   stick

Listen to the words and copy them, writing the main stess in capital letters. On which half of the noun does the stress usually fall?

WRITING

Think of an interesting room and describe it.
PARAGRAPH 1: Say which room you have chosen and where it is. Mention its size and its position in the house.
PARAGRAPH 2: Describe what it looks like: the colours, the furniture and any ornaments and flowers.
PARAGRAPH 3: Describe the atmosphere of the room and how you feel when you are in it.

EXAMPLE
The room I am going to describe is my grandmother's sitting room in her cottage in Wales. It's quite a large room on the ground floor.

The colours of the room are very warm. The wallpaper is . . . There are lots of . . .

There is a fire burning in the fireplace, even in summer, so the room is always warm and cosy. I love . . .

Check

1 Write the correct form of the verbs in brackets, using the present simple or present continuous tenses.

1 Could you sit down, please? I can't see what he (do).
Could you sit down, please? I can't see what he's doing.

2 She (cycle) five miles to school and back every day.
3 The children (start) French at school next year.
4 He (not like) coffee with sugar.
5 I never (work) at the weekend.

6 They (travel) round the United States at the moment.
7 Ssh! I can't hear what she (say).
8 You (speak) Spanish as well as French?
9 I (try) to teach my brother to drive.
10 She (hate) working in the centre of the city.

2 Copy and complete the boxes with the correct form of the verb.

Present	Past
buy	bought
go	
	won
	ran
take	
	gave
come	
tell	
	said
lose	

Present	Past
do	
make	
	saw
bring	
	spoke
read	
know	
	forgot
steal	
	found

3 Choose the correct verb tense and then rewrite the sentences.

1 While I *was having/had* breakfast this morning, my sister phoned from Mexico.
While I was having breakfast this morning, my sister phoned from Mexico.

2 When I *was seeing/saw* his face, I *was realising/realised* my mistake.
3 It *was raining/rained* hard this morning when I *was waking/woke* up.
4 I *was writing/wrote* a letter to my Italian penfriend last night.
5 I *was taking/took* an umbrella because it *was raining/rained*.
6 It was a cold winter night. It *was snowing/snowed* hard and I *was wanting/wanted* to get back home quickly.

4 Write sentences choosing the correct form of *used to* and *be used to*.

1 (I'm not used to/I didn't use to) getting up early. I'm not used to getting up early.

2 (Are you used to/Did you use to) live near here?
3 (I'm used to/I used to) English food.
4 (Did you use to/Are you used to) wear glasses?
5 (I used to/I wasn't used to) doing my own washing.
6 (She's used to/She used to) living in a hot climate.

7 (She didn't use to/She isn't used to) eat any vegetables.
8 (He's used to/He used to) driving a sports car.
9 (Didn't they use to/Weren't they used to) use this park for football training?
10 (She didn't use to/She isn't used to) speaking Spanish with her English husband.

5 Complete the text by inserting one of the verb phrases below.

not allowed to   has to   have to
not supposed to   didn't have to
was allowed to

I've got a new job as a security guard and it's a big change. We . . (have to) . . clock in at 7.30 but in my last job we . . . start until eight o'clock. Also in my last job I . . . take an afternoon off every two weeks but here we don't get any half days. They're strict about smoking too but I think that's good. We're . . . smoke anywhere in the building. Anyone who wants to smoke . . . go outside. But they're not so strict about the lunch hour. We're . . . take more than an hour off but everyone does. Nobody seems to mind very much if you're a bit late back.

6 Write a sentence about each of the following:

1 a sport you enjoy doing
  I enjoy swimming.

2 two things you do every morning
3 what you are wearing at the moment
4 three things you did yesterday
5 what you were doing at nine o'clock
  last night
6 something you used to like doing when
  you were younger
7 something you weren't allowed to do
  at school
8 something that you're not supposed to
  do in your English class (but which you
  sometimes do).

7 Choose the best sentence or expression.

1 In a music store you want to buy the new Pink Floyd compact disc.
  a) I want the new Pink Floyd compact disc.
  b) Have you got the new Pink Floyd compact disc?
  c) Give me the new Pink Floyd compact disc.

2 You decide not to buy the new Pink Floyd compact disc.
  a) I think I'll leave it, thanks. It's not the one I want.
  b) I don't want it.
  c) I'm leaving it.

3 You knock someone's bag by accident while you are leaving the music store.
  a) Sorry!
  b) Never mind.
  c) I really am sorry. I'll get you another one.

8 Reorder the conversation.

Number the following lines in the correct order to make a conversation between a customer and a sales assistant in a stationery shop.

EXAMPLE
1 B Can I help you?

  A What about these then? They're Italian. They come in several pastel colours.
  B Can I help you?
  C Yes, we have. We've got some in red, green, yellow . . . or were you looking for a special colour?
  D O.K. Fine. Next please.
  E Yes, have you got any pencil holders?
  F Yes, they are nice but the colour's not quite right. I think I'll leave it.
  G Well, actually I'd like something pastel to match my room.

9 Agree or disagree with the following statements. Use *So do I* or *Nor do I* to agree, and *I do* or *I don't* to disagree.

1 I honestly think he's mad. (Agree)
  So do I.

2 I don't like people who smoke without asking permission. (Agree)
3 I don't think boxing is a proper sport. (Disagree)
4 I think there should be more women police. (Agree)
5 I think she's wasting her time at that school. (Disagree)
6 I don't think it's right to close the library early on Saturday. (Disagree)

10 What would you say in the following situations?

1 You are at the box office at the theatre. You would like to see the ballet 'Romeo and Juliet' tonight. Ask if they have any tickets left.

2 Your alarm clock didn't go off this morning so you missed the bus and arrived very late for class. Apologise and explain why you were late.

3 You ask to see a mug in a souvenir shop. When the assistant shows it to you, you realise you don't like the design. Decide not to buy it and thank the assistant.

4 Your friend breaks one of your glasses by accident and apologises. The glasses are not valuable. What do you say?

5 Someone lights up a cigarette on the underground train. There is a no-smoking sign on the window. What do you say to the person who's smoking?

Use your English

1 (Student B: page 126)
Describe this scene at a party to Student B. Say what the people are doing and wearing. Student B has a similar picture but there are eight differences between the two pictures. Listen carefully when Student B tells you what the people are doing in his/her picture.

2 (Student B: page 126)
Read out sentences 1–4 to Student B and ask him/her to complete each of them in turn. Start now.

1 The reason I was late was because …
2 I was cycling along the other day when suddenly …
3 When I opened the door of the fridge, …
4 A burglar broke into my flat while …

Now you complete Student B's sentences. Choose the best ending from the sentences below.

5 … the lecturer was still speaking.
6 … he turned round and walked off.
7 … the hot water ran out.
8 … the stage collapsed.

3 Look at the list of polite reminders below. Write answers to the prompts using *supposed to*.

Polite reminders
Please remember that you are a guest in a family so:
– be punctual for all meals
– always keep your room tidy
– no loud music after ten o'clock
– if you go out for the evening please be back by midnight

EXAMPLE
1 A: Why don't you come for a coffee with us?
   B: *I'd better not. It's nearly 6.30 and I'm supposed to be punctual for meals.*
2 A: Come on. We're going to be late for the cinema. Just leave your clothes where they are.
   B: …
3 A: I've got the latest U2 album. Shall I bring it along to your room later on tonight?
   B: …
4 A: Oh well, why don't we go to the late performance of *Malice*? It starts at 11 p.m.
   B: …

4 In pairs, think of a suitable statement using a form of the verb *be used to* to match the pictures.

5 Read the following poem.

He used to dream
of a loving partner
He used to dream
of a woman who would really listen to him
He used to dream
of going places
and of a never-ending dream time
together,
but all he wants right now
is someone to help with the washing up.

Now see if you can write a poem of your own, starting with the same words. You may use *I*, *he*, *she* or *they* if you prefer.

I used to dream …
I used to dream …
I used to dream …
and of …
but all I want right now
is …

Progress test

Units 1–10

GRAMMAR

1 Choose the correct answer.

1 A: What's her address?
   B: I don't know, but her parents ...
      at 3, Grantham Place, Cambridge.

   a) live   b) are living   c) will live

2 A: Any news of Simon?
   B: Yes, he ... with a youth orchestra to Prague at
      the moment.

   a) travels   b) 's travelling   c) will travel

3 A: Have you got the latest Phil Collins album?
   B: Yes, I ... .

   a) do   b) have   c) got

4 A: What does that sign say?
   B: It says that ... to smoke on the underground.

   a) you are not allowed   b) it is not allowed
   c) they do not allow

5 A: Is it all right if I use the phone?
   B: Well, you ... to use it.

   a) 're not suppose   b) 're not allowed
   c) 're not supposed

6 A: Who was that on the telephone?
   B: I don't know. It ... ringing just as I picked it
      up.

   a) was stopping   b) stopped   c) did stop

7 A: When did you see the accident?
   B: ... I was walking through the park.

   a) During   b) While   c) As soon as

8 A: Tell me more about your career so far.
   B: Well, after ... to college, I got a job with a
      recording company.

   a) go   b) gone   c) going

9 A: What do you think of the Beatles?
   B: Well, I ... them a lot but I'm bored with them
      now.

   a) used to like   b) used to liking   c) use to like

10 A: How do you like your job on the farm?
   B: It's fine but I ... at six o'clock.

   a) am not used to wake up
   b) am not used to waking up
   c) used to wake up

VOCABULARY

2 Choose the correct word.

1 How many ... did you get for your composition?
   a) marks   b) degrees   c) grades   d) points

2 Am I allowed to ... the test if I'm under
   eighteen?
   a) pass   b) succeed   c) make   d) take

3 He did very well at college and managed to ...
   into Harvard Business School.
   a) go   b) get   c) pass   d) arrive

4 Do you want a ... to show that you've paid for
   the goods?
   a) bill   b) account   c) receipt   d) reckoning

5 What's the ... of installing a new radiator?
   a) price   b) cost   c) charge   d) amount

6 Is there somewhere where I can ... this dress,
   please?
   a) try on   b) try   c) prove   d) attempt

7 I won't take a taxi, I'll ... the next bus.
   a) wait   b) expect   c) attend   d) wait for

8 I ... my first job as if it were yesterday.
   a) reminisce   b) remind   c) remember
   d) memorise

9 This town is not an ideal place to ... children.
   a) grow   b) grow up   c) bring up   d) raise up

10 You can get almost anything from our village ... .
   a) shop   b) magazine   c) boutique
   d) store room

USAGE

**3 Complete each of the numbered gaps in the
text with a word from the list below.**

very   take   up   asked   way   landed   my   to
hundred   praying   still   which

Schoolboy Tim Burnet was one of three ...(1)...
passengers on board a PANAM jet ...(2)... was
struck by lightning on its ...(3)... to New York. The
ten-year-old said: 'Everyone was ...(4)... frightened.
Babies were crying and people were ...(5)... . We had
to ...(6)... our shoes off and lean forward. I could feel
...(7)... stomach going down like I was on a
fairground ride. When we ...(8)... everybody clapped
and started ...(9)... sing. They were all really happy.'
When ...(10)... if he ever wanted to fly again, the
brave schoolboy said 'Yes, I ...(11)... want to be a
pilot when I grow ...(12)... because if anything like
this ever happened again, I would know the signals.'

-11-
Angie

A motorcycle courier

Most people hate traffic jams but not nineteen-year-old Angie Griffin. Angie is a motorcycle courier whose job involves delivering important packages and letters to different parts of London. She actually enjoys the day-to-day battle with the London traffic, especially the thrill of getting somewhere fast. She likes being a courier even though some people think it is not a very suitable job for a woman.

'I can't understand what they're talking about,' says Angie. 'The only trouble is they don't pay me enough! I'm going to ask for a rise next month.'

Angie was born and brought up in London. She lives with her mother in the rapidly developing dockland area of the East End.

'Everyone is moving here now. It's full of yuppies and BMWs. It'll be like Manhattan in a few years' time, full of skyscrapers. My mum says the cost of living is going up so much we won't be able to live here much longer.'

When Angie is not at work she is a bit of a fitness fanatic. She belongs to a health club and goes there regularly after work.

'I'd like to get a job connected with sport. I'm certainly not going to be a courier for ever. Sometimes I dream of being a sports photographer or a journalist. I often tell my mum: "One day, when I'm rich and famous, I'll buy you a house in the country." But all she really wants is to be able to stay where she is in the East End of London! I can't understand that. I want to get out and do something with my life.'

Glossary
yuppies (coll) young urban professional people with high incomes and fashionable lifestyles.
Manhattan the fashionable centre of New York City, famous for its skyscrapers

Words to learn

courier   traffic jam   deliver   package
suitable   rise   brought (bring) up
develop   go up   fanatic

1 Read and answer.

1 What does Angie's job involve?
2 What does she like about it?
3 What is she going to do next month?
4 Where does she live?
5 What does she do in her spare time?
6 What sort of job does she dream of doing in the future?
7 What does she want to buy for her mother?
8 How is Angie different from her mother?

2 Read and think.

1 Why do some people think that Angie's job is not suitable for a woman?
2 What advantage do motorcyclists have in traffic?
3 Why is the cost of living going up in the dockland area?
4 Why do you think Angie doesn't want to be a courier for ever?

3 About you

1 When and where are the worst traffic jams in your city or in a city near you?
2 Are there any rapidly developing areas near you? Name some.

VOCABULARY

Many names for jobs and occupations end in the suffixes *er, or,* or *ist,* e.g: *photographer, actor, journalist.*

1 Complete the following with the correct suffix *er, or,* or *ist* to make names of jobs and occupations. Use your dictionary to help you. Add similar words of your own.

EXAMPLE: painter

paint-	scient-	pharmac-
telephon-	inspect-	danc-
plumb-	butch-	physic-
reception-	survey-	wait-
solicit-	typ-	jewell-
doct-	carpent-	dent-

2 🖭 Now listen and copy the words, writing the stressed syllable in capital letters.

EXAMPLE
PAINTer   teLEPHonist

TALKING POINT

Give examples of jobs which some people think may be unsuitable for men or women. Say what *you* think and discuss your reasons in groups. The following expressions may be useful:

What about a butcher, for example?
Why shouldn't a woman be a butcher?

Take a butcher, for example.
There's absolutely no reason why a butcher can't be a woman.

ABOUT BRITAIN

The development of London's Docklands

The dockland area in the East End of London used to be, as the name suggests, a busy port. Ships from all over the world docked and unloaded cargo there. After the 1960s the London docks went into decline. The docks were too small to handle the large modern container ships and the loading and unloading facilities were out of date.

However, since the 1980s, a new dockland has developed in the East End, with modern offices and homes, marinas, a new railway system and even a small airport. The old EastEnders say that rich newcomers are pushing up house prices and the cost of living. Their message is: 'Yuppies — Go back where you came from.'

🖭 LISTENING

Listen to Doris, a fruit and vegetable stall holder in Docklands, talking about the changes she sees around her.

Note down complaints she makes.

-12-

Grammar

Future tenses:
going to and *will*

What's the difference in meaning?

1 I'm going to phone him in the morning.
2 I'll phone him in the morning.

Look back at the text about Angie in Unit 11 and notice the other ways in which *going to* and *will/won't* are used. Check the Focus section below to see if you know the different uses of the two tenses.

FOCUS

'Going to'

This tense is used

- to talk about planned decisions and intentions:
  I'm going to ask for a rise next month.

- to talk about future arrangements:
  He's going to stay with us for a week.

- to make predictions about the immediate future when there is some evidence to show what is going to happen:
  Look at those black clouds. It's going to rain in a minute.

'Will'

This tense is used

- to make predictions about the future:
  The Docklands will be like Manhattan in a few years' time.
  We won't be able to live here much longer.

- to make statements of fact about the future:
  Steve will be thirty next birthday.

- to make a decision at the moment of speaking:
  I'll tell him tonight.

- to make a promise or offer:
  I'll post those letters for you.

- with clauses of condition and time:
  If/When I'm rich, I'll buy you a house in the country.

PRACTICE

1 In pairs, practise the following dialogue several times, choosing different words and phrases each time.

A: What are you going to do tomorrow?

B: We're going to spend the day
in the country.
in the mountains.
by the lake.
on the coast.

A: Well, they say it's going to
rain.
be cold.
freeze.
be very windy.
snow.
be lovely and sunny.

B: In that case I'll take my
skis.
swimming things.
skates.
anorak.
shorts.
thick jacket.
raincoat.

2 Find out:

1 what your friends are going to do this weekend.
2 what your teacher is going to do immediately after this lesson.
3 if anyone is going to change their schools or move home in the near future.
4 the weather forecast for tomorrow. Is it going to be warm and sunny or wet and cold?

3 Match the words and phrases in the two columns below to talk about your arrangements for the coming weekend.

EXAMPLE
1 I'm going to write some letters.

1	write	my room
2	phone	some letters
3	do	my bike
4	repair	a cake
5	buy	my girl/boyfriend
6	take back	last week's homework
7	tidy	a new pair of jeans
8	make	my library books

Now add some plans of your own.

4 Exchange the lists above with your partner. Imagine that it is now Monday morning. Admit that you forgot to do each activity and decide when you intend to do it, using will.

EXAMPLE
A: Did you write any letters?
B: No, I forgot but I'll write some tomorrow morning/afternoon/evening.

▣ LISTENING

1 Listen to Angie talking to a friend of hers, Colin.

Note down:
why Angie phones Colin.
why Colin can't come.
what he suggests.
what he offers to do.

2 Listen again and complete the dialogue with the correct form of *going to, will* or the present continuous.

ANGIE: Colin? It's Angie.
COLIN: Oh, hi Angie! How are things?
ANGIE: O.K, thanks. Listen, (1) . . . anything on Saturday?
COLIN: Saturday? I'm not sure. Why?
ANGIE: Well, it's the international athletics meeting at Crystal Palace. I've got two tickets. I think it (2) . . . good. Do you want to come?
COLIN: It sounds fun. (3) . . . my diary. Hang on.
ANGIE: O.K.
COLIN: Let's see. Oh, that's a pity!
ANGIE: What's wrong?
COLIN: (4). . . in a college football match that afternoon, I'm afraid.
ANGIE: That's a shame! Who else can I ask?
COLIN: You could ask Mike. He's quite keen on athletics.
ANGIE: Yes, O.K. What's his number?
COLIN: I can't remember. But I know he's (5) . . . at college this afternoon. (6) . . . him to phone you.
ANGIE: Fine. I (7) . . . home about nine.
COLIN: O.K.
ANGIE: Thanks. Look, I'd better go. I (8) . . . late for work if I'm not careful. Bye for now!
COLIN: Bye Angie!

Practise reading your completed dialogue with your partner.

WRITING

Write the note to Mike which Colin leaves on the college notice board to tell him about Angie's phone call.

Start like this:

Dear Mike,
Sorry I missed you but I've got a message from Angie. She's got . . . I can't go myself because . . . so she wondered if you . . .

-13-

Communication

Requests

Look at the photograph below and answer the questions.

1 What is the receptionist giving Angie?
2 What is Angie going to do?
3 What do you think the receptionist is saying to Angie?

🖥 DIALOGUE

RECEPTIONIST: Could you take this to the Computer Centre in Allington Street, please?
ANGIE: Where's that?
RECEPTIONIST: It's off Buckingham Palace Road.
ANGIE: Right. That'll be £12.50 . . . Thanks. That's £2.50 change.
RECEPTIONIST: Could I have a receipt?
ANGIE: Yes, sure.
RECEPTIONIST: Thank you. And do you think you could hurry? It is rather urgent.
ANGIE: Yes, I'll do my best, but it is the rush hour.
RECEPTIONIST: By the way, would you mind asking them to call me as soon as they get it?
ANGIE: O.K.
RECEPTIONIST: Thanks very much.

Listen and answer the questions.

1 What does the receptionist want Angie to do?
2 How much does she give Angie?
3 What does she ask Angie for?
4 What time of day do you think it is?
5 How many requests are there in the dialogue?

FOCUS

Polite requests

- Asking for things:
  Could I have a receipt?
  Do you think I could have a receipt?

- Asking people to do things:
  Could you take this to the Computer Centre, please?
  Do you think you could hurry?
  Would you mind asking them to call me?

- Agreeing to do things:
  O.K.
  Yes, sure.
  Yes, certainly.
  Yes, of course.
  Yes, I'll do that.

Note

1 *Would you mind . . .,* is more formal.
2 *Please* is not always necessary if a polite intonation is used.

PRACTICE

1 Write a suitable caption for each of the pictures above, using a request each time.

2 You are staying as a paying guest with a British family. In pairs, decide what you would say in the following situations.

1 You would like an extra pillow on your bed.
2 You ask a ten-year-old in the family to post your letters.
3 You don't like coffee. Ask for tea without milk for breakfast.
4 You forget your keys. When you arrive home the house is empty. You go next door and ask to use the telephone to phone your host at work.
5 You would like your teacher to sign an application form for a student travel card.

WRITING

You are ill in bed with flu. Write a note to your English teacher. Explain that you can't come to class for a few days. Say you would like to do some homework while you are away. Ask your teacher to tell a friend in your class what you should do. Say you are also enclosing an application form for a student travel card and ask your teacher to sign it. Say when you hope to be back in class.

▭ LISTENING

Before you listen

What do the following words have in common?
street   square   gardens
lane   avenue   road

Listen

A client calls a courier office with a request. Listen and note the name and address of the client, the delivery address and the cost.

ACT IT OUT

You want a taxi to take you to different places in London. Act out a conversation with the taxi driver. Use the dialogue with Angie and the information below to help you. Include different forms of polite requests in your conversation.

YOU	TAXI DRIVER
Ask the taxi driver to take you to your destination.	
	Ask where it is.
Say which street it is in.	
	Say that you know the street.
Ask the driver to hurry because you are late for an appointment.	
	Say it's rush hour but you'll try.
Ask the cost of the journey.	
	Say the amount.
Pay the driver and ask for a receipt.	
	Give a receipt.
Ask the driver to help you with your suitcase.	
	Agree to do so.
Thank the taxi driver.	

Cynthia could never fully understand . . .

. . . the joys of riding . . .

-14-

Grammar

Ability and possibility:
can, *could* and *be able to*

FOCUS

'Can'/'could'

These are used

- to talk about ability:
  She can sing well but she can't read music.
  When I was young, I could dance quite well but I'm hopeless now.

- to talk about possibility:
  I can come on Monday.
  She couldn't go to the party because she was ill.

- with certain verbs that do not usually occur in the present continuous tense, e.g. *remember, understand, smell, hear, feel, taste, see:*
  I can/could smell something burning.
  I can't understand anything.

'Be able to'

This is used

- to give emphasis to a statement of ability or possibility:
  After her illness she wasn't able to walk for a year.
  We won't be able to live here much longer.
  The use of *couldn't* and *can't* in these two examples would be correct but less forceful.

- to express the meaning of *manage to* or *succeed in* concerning one specific occasion:
  Although the sea was rough, they were able to (= managed to) *swim to the shore.*
  Luckily they heard the alarm and were able to escape.
  Here the use of *could* would not be correct.

- to replace the infinitive and the 'missing' tenses (e.g. the present perfect) of *can* and *could:*
  I'd love to be able to sing well.
  She hasn't been able to get tickets for the concert.

- on formal occasions (especially when written):
  I am afraid we are unable to offer you a refund on your ticket.

Note

1 *Couldn't* (but not *could*) is possible in all situations.
2 The negative of *able to* is *not able to* or *unable to*.

PRACTICE

1 In pairs, use the phrases below to make and respond to requests.

EXAMPLE

A: Could you help me with my project some time this week?

B: I'm afraid I can't this week but I might be able to help you next week.

REQUEST	TIME	ALTERNATIVE
help me with my project	some time this week	next week
come to lunch	on Tuesday	on Wednesday
help me buy a new suit	next week	the week after
look at my computer	this weekend	next weekend
translate a letter	this evening	tomorrow evening

2 Complete the sentences with *can, could* or *be able to*. Sometimes more than one answer is possible.

1 Oh dear, I (not) . . . remember her address.
2 I used to . . . wiggle my ears but I can't any more.
3 Where are the keys? I (not) . . . find them last night.
4 She's moved to York so she will . . . see her parents more often.
5 The theatre seats were awful. We (not) . . . see the stage.
6 The show is very popular but luckily I . . . get two seats for Saturday.
7 My car broke down and I haven't . . . drive it for a week.
8 The exam was easy. I . . . do all the questions.
9 It's nice . . . sleep late on Sundays.
10 My sister (not) . . . swim until she was eleven.
11 After the accident he (not) . . . smell or taste anything.
12 I lost all my money but fortunately I . . . borrow some from friends.

ACT IT OUT

Act out the following situation in pairs. Use the grammar you learnt in Unit 12 as well as in this unit.

A

You have decided you are going to spend a year abroad. You have some savings in the bank but you would like to borrow £500 from your parents. Try and persuade your parents to lend you the money. Decide how and when you intend to pay them back.

B

Your daughter/son wants to borrow £500 so she/he can spend a year abroad. You are not too keen on the idea. You want to know where she/he is going, where she/he is going to live and what she/he is going to do. You also want to know how and when you will get your money back.

WRITING

Write a letter inviting some English-speaking guests to the theatre.

PARAGRAPH 1

Explain that you were able to get tickets for a popular show. Say which show and when the performance is.

PARAGRAPH 2

Apologise and explain that you won't be able to meet them at their hotel and ask them to meet you at the theatre instead.

PARAGRAPH 3

Ask them to telephone you to say if they can come or not. Say where you will be and when they can contact you.

(Your address)
(the date)

Dear . . .,
After our conversation last week, I telephoned the theatre and luckily I . . . tickets for . . . on . . . and I hope you . . .

I'm afraid I won't . . . because . . . so . . .
Could you . . . I'll be . . .
With best wishes,

Yours sincerely,

. . . until she was finally able to control her horse.

BLACKBERRIES

by Leslie Norris

'There, I think that's enough,' said Mr Frensham. 'Very handsome.'

The boy was having his hair cut for the first time in his life. 'We're off to do some shopping,' the boy's mother said as she handed Mr Frensham the money.

They were going to buy the boy a cap, a round cap with a little button on top and a peak over his eyes. The boy wanted the cap very much.

'This is the smallest size we have,' the man in the clothes shop said. He put the cap on the boy's head and stood back to look. It was a beautiful cap.

'It's a little big,' said the man, 'but you want something he can grow into, something that will last him a long time.'

'Oh I hope so,' his mother said. 'It's expensive enough.'

The boy carried the cap back to the house himself.

When his father came home late in the afternoon, the boy put on his cap and stood before his father. The man put his hand on the boy's head and looked at him.

'On Sunday,' he said, 'we'll go for a walk. Just you and I. We'll be men together.'

Although it was late in September, the sun was warm and the paths were dry. 'Come on,' said his father, 'or we'll never reach Fletcher's Woods.'

'Will there be blackberries there?' he asked.

'There should be,' his father said. 'I'll pick some for you.'

In Fletcher's Woods his father showed him a tangle of blackberry bushes. Clusters of purple fruit hung in the branches. His father reached up and chose a blackberry for him. Its skin was plump and shining.

'You can eat it,' his father said.

Together they picked and ate the dark berries, until their lips were purple and their hands marked and scratched.

'We should take some for your mother,' the man said.

They had nothing to carry them in, so the boy put his new cap next to the grass and they filled it with berries.

🌿 🌿 🌿

'It was a stupid thing to do,' his mother said, 'utterly stupid. What were you thinking of?'

The man did not answer.

'If we had the money, it would be different,' his mother said. 'Where do you think the money comes from?'

'I know where it comes from,' his father said. 'I work hard enough for it.'

The cap lay on the table. Inside it was wet with the sticky juice of blackberries. The stains were dark and irregular.

'It'll dry out all right,' his father said.

His mother's face was red and her voice was shrill.

'If you had a proper job,' she shouted, 'and could buy caps by the dozen, then ...'

'I do what I can,' he said.

'That's not much,' his mother said. 'You don't do much!'

Appalled, the child watched the quarrel grow. He began to cry quietly, to himself, knowing that it was a different weeping from any that he had experienced before, that he was crying for a different pain. And he began to understand that they were different people; his father, his mother, himself, and that he must learn sometimes to be alone.

44

Reading

Before you read

Look at the illustration. Think about the questions.
1 What are the man and the boy doing?
2 How old is the boy?
3 Do you think he's enjoying himself? Why?

Guess the meaning

peak path tangle cluster plump shrill
quarrel appalled

COMPREHENSION

1 Choose the best answer a), b) or c).

1 The mother decided to take the cap although it
   was a little big because:
   a) it would last him longer.
   b) the larger size looked good on the boy.
   c) when his hair grew longer, the cap would fit
      better.
2 The boy liked the cap because:
   a) it was a nice colour.
   b) it covered his hair which was now too short.
   c) it made him look more grown-up.
3 The boy enjoyed his Sunday walk with his
   father because:
   a) he had never been to Fletcher's Woods
      before.
   b) they picked and ate blackberries together.
   c) he could wear his new cap.
4 The mother was very angry because:
   a) they got back late.
   b) they had eaten most of the blackberries.
   c) they had collected blackberries in the boy's
      new cap.
5 The mother was very upset because:
   a) the cap had cost her a lot of money and was
      ruined.
   b) the boy didn't want to wear the cap again.
   c) her husband didn't have a job.

2 Retell the story using the prompts.

One day a mother and her young son went to the
   hairdresser's to have the boy's hair cut.
Afterwards, his mother …
Unfortunately the cap … but the mother …
When he got home, the boy …
The father promised …
On the walk, his father showed him …
They picked …
They decided to … so …
When they got home …
The little boy …

THINK ABOUT IT

1 What does the story tell you about the boy's
   relationship with his father?
2 What do you think the quarrel was really about?
3 What does the phrase 'crying for a different
   pain' mean?
4 What lesson do you think the boy has learnt
   about life? Do you think it is a good or
   necessary lesson to learn?

ABOUT YOU

1 Are you an only child or are you part of a big
   family?
2 Who did you feel closer to as a child, your
   mother or your father?
3 What interesting things do you remember
   from your childhood?

VOCABULARY

Which of the verbs below can be used with which nouns?

EXAMPLE
mark: cup, clothes, …

VERBS
mark scratch spoil stain soak crack
tear ruin

NOUNS
hands cup clothes mirror armchair
performance evening

WRITING

Write a quarrel between a brother and a sister:
the sister has borrowed the brother's jeans jacket
without asking and has torn it.

Start like this:
BROTHER: By the way, have you seen my jeans
          jacket?

Grammar

First conditional and time clauses

Look at the pictures and answer the questions.

1 What will they do if it rains?

2 What will happen if she bends her knees more?

3 What will happen if he's late again?

In which sentence is the speaker doing the following:

giving advice?
talking about a possible future event?
giving a warning?

Which verb tense is used in the *if* clause and which verb tense in the main clause?

FOCUS

The first conditional: 'if' clauses + future

This structure is used

- to describe a possible future event and its consequences:
  If it starts to rain, we'll play inside.

- to give advice:
  If you bend your knees, you'll keep your balance better.

- to warn or threaten:
  If you're late again, you won't be in the team!

Time clauses with 'when' and 'as soon as'

- In time clauses, *as soon as* means *immediately*, but *when* is not so definite:
  I'll phone you as soon as I get home. (immediately)
  I'll phone you when I get home. (not so definite)

Points to note

- In certain cases, *will/won't* can be replaced by *going to*:
  If you're not home by six, I'm going to eat without you.

- *Unless* can replace *if . . . not* to add emphasis.
  If you don't go now, you'll miss the train.
  Unless you go now, you'll miss the train.

- The future tense is used in the main clause, but not in first conditional or time clauses.

- *Will/won't* can be replaced by certain modals, e.g. *may, can.*
  If it rains, we may go to the cinema.

What's the difference in meaning?

1 If I see Jan, I'll tell her about the match.
2 When I see Jan, I'll tell her about the match.

PRACTICE

1 Rewrite the sentences making the *if* clause negative. Make any necessary changes to the main clause to keep the same meaning.

EXAMPLE

1 If you work hard, you'll pass your exams.
  If you don't work hard, you won't pass your exams.

2 If you go to the market early, you'll get some fresh fish.
3 If you hurry, you'll catch the bus.
4 If I sell my car, I'll be able to afford a holiday.
5 If it's sunny, we'll go to the beach.
6 If I get a residence permit, I'll be able to stay in the USA.

2 Look at the sentences in Exercise 1 again. Rewrite them using *unless*.

EXAMPLE

You won't pass your exams unless you work hard.

3 Reply to the questions on the left choosing from the list on the right. Start with *I'll/We'll . . . as soon as . . .*

EXAMPLE

1 When are we going to eat?
b) We'll eat as soon as John gets back.

1 When are we going to eat?
2 When are you going to do your homework?
3 Aren't you going to leave soon?
4 When can you lend me that book?
5 When are you going to come and visit us?
6 When are you going to finish that report?

a) I finish reading it.
b) John gets back.
c) I get a free weekend.
d) this programme finishes.
e) I get my typewriter back.
f) the babysitter arrives.

4 Complete the conversation between Angie and her mother by writing the correct form of the verb in brackets.

MOTHER: I'm off to work now. What time will you be back?
ANGIE: About six. But I (ring) you if there (be) any problems.
MOTHER: Well, if you (be) back before me, you (have to) get something for supper.
ANGIE: O.K, I (decide) on something when I (get) to the supermarket.
MOTHER: If I (pass) a greengrocer's, I (buy) some strawberries.
ANGIE: Great!
MOTHER: Is Colin coming round tonight?
ANGIE: He didn't say but if he (get in touch), I (invite) him to supper.
MOTHER: Look at the time. I (miss) the bus unless I (go) now.
ANGIE: O.K. Bye. I (see) you when I (get) home.

5 In pairs or groups, complete these 'tips and hints'.

EXAMPLE

1 Your T-shirts won't shrink if . . .
  Your T-shirts won't shrink if you dry them naturally.

2 You'll get a smoother shave if . . .
3 If . . ., you'll tan more quickly.
4 If . . ., your skin may go dry.
5 Your roses will last longer if . . .
6 Your house plants will die unless . . .
7 Your car won't use so much petrol if . . .

6 Discuss your advice with your partner and the rest of the class. In pairs, write down three useful tips that you know.

🔊 LISTENING

Before you listen

Identify the following parts of the body:

back   head   arms   feet
fist   shoulder   mouth   nose

Listen

Listen to an interview with a trainer who gives advice on how to run properly. What advice does he give about the correct position of your body, your back, your head and your arms, and what does he advise about breathing?

WRITING

Write a short list of Dos and Don'ts for running, or another sport you know well, and give explanations for your advice.

EXAMPLE
DO
Wear comfortable shoes.
If you don't, you'll get blisters.

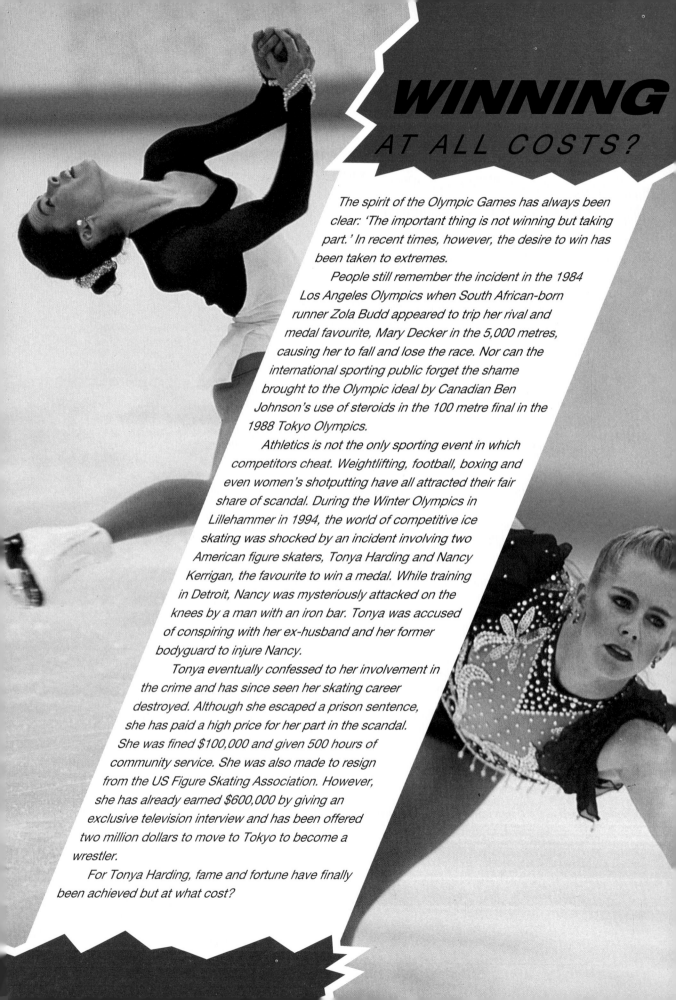

WINNING
AT ALL COSTS?

The spirit of the Olympic Games has always been clear: 'The important thing is not winning but taking part.' In recent times, however, the desire to win has been taken to extremes.

People still remember the incident in the 1984 Los Angeles Olympics when South African-born runner Zola Budd appeared to trip her rival and medal favourite, Mary Decker in the 5,000 metres, causing her to fall and lose the race. Nor can the international sporting public forget the shame brought to the Olympic ideal by Canadian Ben Johnson's use of steroids in the 100 metre final in the 1988 Tokyo Olympics.

Athletics is not the only sporting event in which competitors cheat. Weightlifting, football, boxing and even women's shotputting have all attracted their fair share of scandal. During the Winter Olympics in Lillehammer in 1994, the world of competitive ice skating was shocked by an incident involving two American figure skaters, Tonya Harding and Nancy Kerrigan, the favourite to win a medal. While training in Detroit, Nancy was mysteriously attacked on the knees by a man with an iron bar. Tonya was accused of conspiring with her ex-husband and her former bodyguard to injure Nancy.

Tonya eventually confessed to her involvement in the crime and has since seen her skating career destroyed. Although she escaped a prison sentence, she has paid a high price for her part in the scandal. She was fined $100,000 and given 500 hours of community service. She was also made to resign from the US Figure Skating Association. However, she has already earned $600,000 by giving an exclusive television interview and has been offered two million dollars to move to Tokyo to become a wrestler.

For Tonya Harding, fame and fortune have finally been achieved but at what cost?

–17–

Topic

Sport

Before you read

1 Have you ever been to the Olympic Games?
2 Which country was host to the last Olympic Games?
3 What are some of the main events in the summer and winter Olympics?
4 How many Olympic champions have come from your country in the last ten years?
5 Do you know of any major scandals involving sports personalities?

Words to learn

at all costs   spirit   cheat (v)
take to extremes   shame (n)
trip (v)   rival   medal   scandal
competitive   iron bar   conspire
confess   prison sentence
fine (v)   resign from   exclusive

1 Read and answer.

1 Read the article on the left. Then copy and complete the chart about the three people involved in sports scandals.

Name	
Nationality	
Sporting event	
City	
Year	
Scandal	

2 How was Tonya Harding punished?
3 How did Tonya gain from her crime?

2 Read and think.

How would you explain the last line of the text?

3 About you

1 How important to you is winning in sports and games?
2 Which sports do you like to watch and which do you like to take part in?

VOCABULARY

1 Look at the words below and find two water sports, two team sports, two winter sports, four indoor sports and two motor sports.

skiing   football   scrambling   ice skating   volleyball   boxing
swimming   windsurfing   motor racing   table tennis   gymnastics
wrestling

2 Match the sporting event with the location.

EXAMPLE: ski slope
A: ski   swimming   athletics   boxing   skating   tennis   golf   football
B: course   pitch   court   track   ring   rink   pool   slope

🔲 LISTENING

Listen to these commentaries and note which sports are taking place.

TALKING POINT

1 Do you think top sports personalities should make such large sums of money?
2 What are the advantages and disadvantages of holding the Olympic Games in your country?

WRITING

Imagine your city or a city near you has been chosen to host the next Olympic Games. You are worried about this decision and want to know how the city is going to raise the money to provide all the necessary extra facilities. Write a letter to a newspaper. Join your ideas with *not only ... but also ...* and *as well as.*

EXAMPLE

Dear Sir,

It has recently been announced that the next Olympics are going to be held in ... .

As a resident of ... I am very worried about this decision. If we hold the Games here, we will not only have build a new ... but also ... several new ... for ... .

The amount of extra traffic will be enormous and, as well as building ..., they will also have to improve ... .

What I would like to know is, how ...?

Yours faithfully,

—18—

Communication

Checking information

📟 DIALOGUE

Angie is talking to Carl, a neighbour.

ANGIE: Hi, Carl! What are you doing here? Aren't you supposed to be at school?

CARL: No, we've got the afternoon off. I wanted to go swimming at the sports centre but the pool's closed all this week.

ANGIE: Isn't there a pool in Lansbury Park?

CARL: Yes, but it's no good. It's too shallow and anyway all the kids go there.

ANGIE: What about the Oasis at Mile End? The 49 bus goes there, doesn't it?

CARL: Yes, but it takes so long.

ANGIE: Come on, lazy bones! I'll take you on the bike. Grab this helmet and jump on!

Listen and answer the questions.

1 Why isn't Carl at school?
2 Why can't he go swimming at the sports centre?
3 Why doesn't he want to go to the pool at Lansbury Park?
4 Why doesn't Carl want to go to the pool at Mile End by bus?
5 What does Angie offer to do?

FOCUS

Checking information

- Checking information:
  Isn't there a pool in Lansbury Park? (negative question)
  The 49 bus goes there, doesn't it? (tag question)

- Checking information with surprise:
  Aren't you supposed to be at school? (negative question)

PRACTICE

1 Rephrase each question in the Focus section using either a negative question or a tag question.

EXAMPLE
There's a pool in Lansbury Park, isn't there?

2 Write some facts about your partner which you are fairly sure about. Then check the facts using a tag question.

EXAMPLE
Notes:
Janine – is French
– lives outside Paris
– works in a bank

Questions:
You're French, aren't you?
You live outside Paris, don't you?

Check the facts again, using a negative question each time.

EXAMPLE
Aren't you French?

3 Indicate surprise in these holiday situations. Use a negative question each time.

EXAMPLE
1 It's 8.30 a.m. on a sunny morning and your friend is still in bed.
Aren't you going to get up?

2 At supper your friend leaves half a plate of chips on the plate.
3 In the morning in the bathroom your friend looks pale and is holding a packet of aspirin.
4 In the sea your friend puts on a pair of inflatable plastic arm bands.
5 At the bank your friend says: 'Where on earth is my passport?'
6 In a beach café you think you recognise an old school friend.

WHEN IS A QUESTION NOT A QUESTION?

The answer to this could be: 'When it's a greeting'. Take 'How do you do?', for example. Although this ends in a question mark, it is not a question but a greeting. The correct response is to repeat the same 'question': 'How do you do?'

And again, if a friend stops you in the street and asks: 'How are you?', remember that this is not a true question. It would be extremely inappropriate to give a long description of your state of health. A simple 'Fine, thanks.' is all they wish to hear, even though you may be wrapped in bandages as you speak.

If someone says at table: 'Could you pass the milk?', they will be very surprised if you answer: 'Yes, I could.' This is not a question but a request. Likewise, 'Couldn't you go and fetch them, James?' sounds like a harmless question but is in fact a direct order to James.

▦ LISTENING

1 Listen to two people who meet in the street.

1 What are their names?
2 What nationality is the man?
3 When did they first meet?
4 Why did he have to leave so quickly?
5 How does the man end the conversation in the street?

2 Listen again and copy down all the questions you heard.

ACT IT OUT

You meet someone in the street whom you think you saw at a party last week. You are fairly sure you remember his/her name. In pairs, act out a conversation. Mention the party and say how much you enjoyed it. Suggest the person comes and has a drink.

Start like this:

YOU: Hello! Didn't we meet at . . .
HE/SHE: Yes, that's right.
YOU: You're . . ., aren't you?

READING

Before you read
How do you answer the questions, *How do you do?* and *How are you?*

Read the text above and answer the questions.

1 How many different examples of questions which are not really questions are mentioned in the text?
2 List all the 'questions' and say what other meaning they have.

EXAMPLE
How do you do? = a greeting

WRITING

Write a paragraph about why you think English is an easy or difficult language to learn. You may like to mention the grammar, the vocabulary, the pronunciation and intonation, the spelling, the idioms or any other aspect which interests you.

Start like this:

I think English is quite a . . . language to learn. For example, . . . Another thing is . . . Also, . . . And finally, . . .

—19—

Grammar

In case

Here. Take this road map in case you get lost.

spare can of petrol

red triangle

road map

spare wheel

First Aid Kit

FOCUS

'In case'

- This structure is used to give the reason for doing something:
  Take this road map in case you get lost.
  The *in case* clause gives the reason for the main clause, i.e. the reason for taking a map.

Points to note

- *In case* cannot be followed by *will* or *going to*. The present tense is used to talk about the future in an *in case* clause:
  You need some coins in case you have to phone.
  Take some coins in case you need to phone.
  I'll take some coins in case I need to phone.

- *In case* can also be used to explain why someone did something in the past:
  She took her umbrella in case it rained.

What's the difference in meaning?

1 I'll buy some apples if I get hungry.
2 I'll buy some apples in case I get hungry.

PRACTICE

1 In pairs, match the items in the picture above with the phrases below to explain why you need certain things in your car.

get lost   break down in the dark
run out of petrol   have an accident
have a puncture

EXAMPLE
You need a spare can of petrol in case you run out (of petrol).

2 How would you use *in case* in these situations?

1 You hear a weather forecast which predicts that it will probably rain in your area just as you leave your home. What do you say?
2 You are talking to an American visitor. When you say goodbye, you give him/her your address. What do you say?

3 Complete these sentences with *if* or *in case*.

1 I'll take a plastic bottle of water . . . I get thirsty.
2 Can you buy me a newspaper . . . you pass a kiosk on your way home?
3 We'll have a swim . . . we see a nice place by the river.
4 I'll change a travellers' cheque . . . the bank is open.
5 He took some extra travellers' cheques . . . he ran out of money.
6 . . . the post office is open, can you buy me some stamps?
7 When you drive to the mountains this winter, put chains on your wheels . . . the roads are icy.

TALKING POINT

In pairs or groups, discuss what precautions concerning injections, money, medical supplies, clothing and equipment you need to take on a trip to one of the following places:

Lapland   The Sahara Desert   The Amazon

🖳 LISTENING

Listen to someone giving advice about a trip to Thailand. Note the advice she gives about luggage, clothes, money and learning the language.

WRITING

Some friends are going to spend a week in your home while you are away. Write a note welcoming them and explaining where and why you have left the following:
extra blankets, spare key, your phone number, your doctor's phone number.

Start like this:

Dear Mark and Jenny,

Welcome to the flat. You will find some extra blankets in the . . . in case . . .

−20−

Reading

Fever Pitch by Nick Hornby *is an account of the writer's lifelong love affair with the London football team, Arsenal. His memories span from 1968 to 1992. He is a full time writer and journalist and lives in Highbury within walking distance of the Arsenal ground.*

Fever Pitch

For a match to be truly memorable back then, the kind of game that sent me home buzzing inside with the fulfilment of it all, these conditions had to be met: I had to go with my dad; we had to eat lunch in the fish and chip shop (sitting down, no sharing of tables); we had to have seats in the Upper West Stand (because you can see down the players' tunnel from there and so can greet the arrival of the team on the pitch before anyone in the ground); Arsenal had to win by two clear goals; the stadium had to be full; the game had to be filmed on television; and Dad had to be wearing warm clothes (he sometimes forgot his coat and then I would feel guilty when he got cold). These were enormous demands, and it is hardly surprising that everything came together just once for a game against Derby in 1972, when Arsenal beat the eventual League Champions 2–0 with two Charlie George goals, one a penalty and the other a superb header. And because there was a table for us in the fish and chip shop, and because my dad remembered his coat, I have allowed this game to become something it wasn't. It now represents for me the whole works, the entire fixation, but that's wrong. Arsenal were too good, Charlie's goal was too spectacular, the crowd was too big and too appreciative of the team's performance. Life isn't, and never has been, a 2–0 home win against the League leaders after a fish-and-chip lunch.

> **Glossary**
> **Charlie George** a famous Arsenal player from the 1970s.

Before you read

1 Do you play or like to watch football?
2 Do you support a particular team?
3 Have you ever watched a football match live? What was the atmosphere like?
4 List as many words as you can think of to do with football.

COMPREHENSION

1 Read the extract and list the seven conditions that had to be met for a game to be truly memorable for the writer.
2 In what ways was the one special occasion he mentions not typical of Arsenal's performance in matches?

THINK ABOUT IT

When the writer says that the crowd was 'too appreciative' of Arsenal's performance, how do you imagine that the crowd usually behaves?

VOCABULARY

1 Find words or expressions in the extract which mean:

1 really
2 narrow passage under the stand
3 brilliant
4 whole
5 obsession
6 amazing
7 ready to praise and applaud

2 Explain the difference between the pairs of words.

pitch/ground
player/team
stand/stadium
fans/crowd
free kick/penalty
to beat/to win
to shoot/to score
to kick/to head

🎧 LISTENING

Listen to the extract from the end of a football match and say:

– which two teams are playing
– who won
– what the final score was

TALKING POINT

What conditions would have to be met for you to remember the following events?

– a summer picnic
– a walk in winter
– an evening out with a special friend

Check

1 Write the correct form of the verbs in brackets, using the *going to* future or the present continuous.

1 I don't know what I (do) with my old computer. Perhaps you'd like it?
2 The plane (leave) at 6 o'clock.
3 I know you (like) our new geography teacher.
4 Come on! We (be) late.
5 Sue and Alan (get) married on Saturday.

6 Take a warm coat. It's very cloudy. I think it (snow).
7 I (take) my driving test on Wednesday.
8 The twins (arrive) on the 11.50 train.
9 I feel terrible. I think I (be) sick.
10 The new boutique (open) on 5th May.

2 Write the correct form of the verbs in brackets, using *will* or *going to*.

1 A: The phone's ringing.
   B: O.K. I (answer) it.

2 A: What (you/do) after supper?
   B: Watch television. Why?

3 A: We've run out of coffee.
   B: Have we? I (get) some more when I go out.

4 A: Have a good time in Italy!
   B: Thanks. I (send) you a postcard.

5 A: When (you/repair) my bike, Mum?
   B: I (do) it tomorrow if I have time.

6 A: Phew! It's hot in here.
   B: Yes, isn't it. I (turn on) the air conditioning.

7 A: Which do you want, the red one or the black one?
   B: I (have) the red one please.

8 A: It's so crowded in here I think I (faint).
   B: I (take) you outside for a while.

3 Write the correct form of the verbs in brackets using *will* or the present simple.

1 When she (hear) her result, she (be) pleased.
2 I (not phone) you unless something important (happen).
3 If he (not come), you (be) upset?
4 They (laugh) when they (realise) it's a trick.
5 I think you (like) Nick when you (meet) him.

6 I (send) you a postcard as soon as I (reach) Paris.
7 I (get) some fresh eggs if they (have) any in the market.
8 (Go) she to college if she (get) good grades in her exams?

4 Match the two halves of the following sentences.

1 If they find out about this
2 Here are some sandwiches
3 I won't call a doctor
4 You'll arrive before lunch
5 Will he take the job
6 It'll taste much nicer
7 Please don't telephone
8 If you soak it in cold water
9 I'll cook the spaghetti
10 I'll buy her some flowers

a) if you catch the 9.00 train.
b) there'll be trouble.
c) if they offer it to him?
d) the stain will come out.
e) in case you get hungry.
f) unless her temperature goes up.
g) when she's had her operation.
h) if you add a little sugar.
i) unless it's urgent.
j) as soon as they arrive.

5 Complete the sentences with *can*, *could* or the correct form of *be able to*. In some sentences more than one answer is possible.

1 If we're lucky we . . . see the whole match.
2 What? She's seven and she . . . (not) tie her shoelaces!
3 I'd like to . . . speak a little bit of every language.
4 I went to the library, Mrs Price, but I . . . (not) find the book you wanted.
5 After trying for many hours, they . . . to rescue the boy.
6 I . . . (not) swim until I was fifteen.

6 Complete the question tags.

1 Janice doesn't like me, . . . ?
2 This is a nice vilage, . . . ?
3 I'm not wrong, . . . ?
4 You couldn't give me a hand, . . . ?
5 They're not telling the truth, . . . ?
6 He's had an accident, . . . ?
7 It rained all week, . . . ?
8 We didn't sell many tickets, . . . ?

7 Choose the odd word out.

1 doctor dentist solicitor physician
2 mark crack scratch pull
3 shoulder heel elbow fist
4 tree court pitch course
5 swimming sailing golf windsurfing
6 hit score kick shoot

8 Join the two parts of the sentences with the words in brackets.

1 She's the director of the company. She's a mother of two young children. (not only . . . but also)
2 I don't like cooking. I don't like washing up. (neither . . . nor)
3 I like giving presents. I like receiving them too. (both . . . and)
4 I enjoy going to concerts. I also enjoy listening to jazz. (as well as)
5 I suggest hiring a video for the evening. Alternatively, we could go to the cinema. (either . . . or)

9 Circle the best answer.

1 A: Tea or coffee?
  B: a) Do you think you could give me some tea please?
    b) Tea please.
    c) I want tea.

2 A: a) Lend me your newspaper, please?
    b) Excuse me, would you mind lending me your newspaper?
    c) Excuse me, can't you lend me your newspaper?
  B: Certainly.

3 A: It's Michael. He's phoning from the airport.
  B: Goodness!
    a) Has he left yet?
    b) Isn't he leaving yet?
    c) Hasn't he left yet?

4 A: a) I went out with Britta yesterday.
  B: I think I know her.
    a) She isn't the girl from the sports shop.
    b) Is she the girl from the sports shop?
    c) Isn't she the girl from the sports shop?
  A: That's right.

5 A: I remember you.
    a) You went to Kent High School, didn't you?
    b) Did you go to Kent High School?
    c) Aren't you going to Kent High School?

10 What would you say in the following situations? Sometimes there is more than one possible answer.

1 Your friend is out when you telephone so you want to leave a message.
2 You have bought a lot of stamps at the post office and you would like a receipt.
3 You are introduced to someone at a party. You are sure you went to school with him.
4 You offer a friend an ice cream but she refuses. Express surprise that she doesn't like ice cream.
5 Ask your teacher politely to give you extra grammar lessons.
6 Your mother returns home early one evening. You thought she was supposed to be at a meeting.
7 You are at a party. Give advice to a friend who spills red wine on a white carpet.
8 Your friend is going on holiday. You remind them to take out insurance.
9 You are going to spend a few days in France. Your friend loves French cheeses. What does the friend say to you?

Use your English

1 (Student B: page 126)
You and Student B each have a list of plans and a list of offers. You start by reading out your first plan and Student B chooses an appropriate offer from his/her list.

EXAMPLE
A: I'm going to give a party on Saturday.
B: I'll help you with the food.

Take it in turns to read out your plans.

Plans
give a party on Saturday
see the latest James Bond film this evening
spend the evening at home
find a holiday job this summer
make some lunch

Offers (for Student B's plans)
come to classes with you
choose a colour for you
dry the dishes
drive you to the bus station
give you my old one

2 In pairs, take it in turns to decide what requests to make in the following situations. Each time the other person should respond either positively or negatively.

1 You need change for a £5 note. You go into a shop.
2 You sit down at a table in café. The ashtray is full of cigarette ends. You call the waitress.
3 You have run out of videos to record programmes from the television. A friend is going into town.
4 Your brother has the latest Sting CD. You would like to record it on to a cassette.
5 You buy a sweater but when you get home you decide that it is the wrong colour. You take it back to the shop.
6 You are listening to some music on the radio with some friends. Suddenly you hear that they are playing your current favourite song.

3 The Wood family are planning a two-week summer holiday. Look at the three holiday advertisements and the Woods' preferences.

Mr Wood: – doesn't like flying
– doesn't like too much sun
Mrs Wood: – likes warm sunny weather
– doesn't want to cook
Cara Wood: – doesn't like staying in hotels
– wants to get a góod tan
Jeff Wood: – likes active holidays
– likes a busy nightlife

SAIL OR WINDSURF
Bored with just the summer sun? Read about our active and exciting holidays in Spain. Novice or expert, by yourself or with friends, one of our wide range of yacht or windsurf holidays will suit you. Non-sailing friends enjoy our colourful resorts. Our hotels are welcoming and we look after small children while parents sail for the day. More details from:
Merlin Sailing, 10 Portsmouth Road, Southport, or ring
0704 9651

LERICI
La Spezia, Italy

Hillside flat with superb sea views. Sleeps 4

Tel: Manchester (061) 784083.

SCOTTISH HIGHLANDS Ullapool picturesque fishing village. Ideal family holidays with magnificent scenery. Beautifully located coastal/inland self-catering cottages on Highland estate. Salmon/trout. Loch fishing. Ponies. SAE Hill's Holidays, Ullapool, 0854 67196.

In pairs, make a separate suggestion for each member of the family, using the following structures:

If you (don't) like ..., you should go to ... because ...
or If you (don't) want to ..., you'll enjoy ... because ...

EXAMPLE
Mr Wood:
If you don't like flying, you should go to Scotland because you can get there by train or car.
If you don't like too much sun, you'll enjoy Scotland because you never get sun every day in Scotland.

Progress test

Units 11–20

GRAMMAR

1 Choose the correct answer.

Carol and Martin are friends at work.

CAROL: Have you got any plans for next weekend?
MARTIN: Yes, I ...(1)... visit my cousins in Scotland.

    a) will   b) 'm going to   c) go to

CAROL: That's a long way to go. Are you going to drive there?
MARTIN: Yes, ...(2)... there's a problem with the car.

    a) if not   b) if   c) unless

CAROL: You've got a Saab, ...(3)...?

    a) haven't you   b) don't you   c) isn't it

MARTIN: That's right.
CAROL: ...(4)... Saabs supposed to be very reliable?

    a) Are   b) Aren't   c) Don't

MARTIN: Not when they're fifteen years old! In fact, I'd better take it in for a service ...(5)... it breaks down on the way.

    a) if   b) in case   c) in case of

CAROL: Well, I hope we get better weather than we're having now. Just look at those clouds. I think it's ...(6)... rain again.

    a) going to   b) will   c) shall

MARTIN: I'd better go. I'll telephone you about those concert tickets as soon as I ...(7)... how much they cost.

    a) will find out   b) am finding out
    c) find out

CAROL: O.K. If they ...(8)... very expensive, Jim probably won't want to go.

    a) shall be   b) 're   c) 'll be

MARTIN: I'll let you know anyway. O.K., I'm off.
CAROL: Oh, would you mind ...(9)... these letters on your way to the station?

    a) posting   b) having posted   c) to post

MARTIN: Fine. ...(10)... finish all of them?

    a) Could you   b) Can you
    c) Were you able to

CAROL: Yes, I was. I'm very pleased.
MARTIN: Great. See you tomorrow.

VOCABULARY

2 Choose the correct word.

1 I'm afraid this dress isn't ... for the occasion.
    a) convenient   b) comfortable   c) suitable

2 Albert Einstein was a famous ... .
    a) doctor   b) physicist   c) physician

3 Her sixteen-year-old daughter is already a very good ... .
    a) cook   b) cooker   c) chef

4 The ... has risen enormously.
    a) cost of living   b) cost of life   c) living cost

5 It was difficult for me to ... this decision.
    a) do   b) make   c) come by

6 I'm afraid I have to ... the afternoon visiting my aunt in hospital.
    a) pass   b) take   c) spend

7 I can't remember what ... before the accident.
    a) passed   b) came to pass   c) happened

8 The footballer was sent off the ... for bad language.
    a) court   b) pitch   c) track

9 She told me to ... the keys from her handbag.
    a) get   b) obtain   c) receive

10 The car was slightly ... in the accident.
    a) damaged   b) hurt   c) destroyed

USAGE

3 Complete each of the numbered gaps in the text with a word from the list below.

taking of pool swim also alone able if for best

Swimming is not only good for your lungs, it is ...(1)... one of the best forms ...(2)... all-round exercise. If you want to use swimming as a way of ...(3)... exercise, you must be ...(4)... to swim steadily ...(5)... at least half a minute. ...(6)... you don't swim very well, lessons will help to improve your technique. The ...(7)... place to swim for exercise is an indoor ...(8)... . The water is calm and warm and you can ...(9)... all the year round and in any weather. There's only one safety rule that everyone should obey – never swim ...(10)... .

21

Stratford-upon-Avon,
Warwickshire,
England

July 15

Dear Lori,
Sorry I haven't written for so long but I've been very busy. As you know, I've been working my way around Europe since I last wrote and I haven't had time to write home.

As you can see from my address, I've finally arrived in Stratford-upon-Avon. It really is a beautiful town, even though it's crawling with tourists. In fact, I've been standing in line at the theater for two hours trying to get a ticket to see 'Hamlet' and I've finally managed to get one. I'm really happy. They say it's a great play.

I'm really happy to be here in this _____ and consider I've been _____ over _____ jus _____

I've just started a temporary job as a waiter in a hotel here. The chef is really strange! He got mad at me because I made a mistake with the breakfast orders and he hasn't stopped persecuting me since. I don't want to get fired. I really need to make some money this summer.

Are you still in NYC or have you managed to get to your place on Long Island yet? I hope the boat wasn't washed away in all those storms I've been hearing about.

I guess I'd better stop and get back to work. Be good and say Hi to the Empire State for me!

Love,
Glenn

P.S. Could you do me a favor and send me a copy of the Village Voice? I want to keep in touch.

Glenn

An American in Britain

Words to learn

finally chef temporary persecute
fired storm do somebody a favour

1 Read and find out:

1 where Glenn is now.
2 why he's feeling pleased.
3 what job he's got.
4 why he doesn't want to lose it.

Glossary
'Hamlet' a famous play by William Shakespeare, who was born in Stratford-upon-Avon
NYC New York City
Long Island a summer resort area just outside the city of New York
The Empire State the Empire State Building, a famous New York landmark
The Village Voice a weekly New York newspaper

2 Number the topics in the order in which they occur in Glenn's letter.

- a description of his job
- his recent travels
- an apology and a reason for not writing earlier
- his opinion of Stratford
- an incident which occurred at work
- an inquiry about life back in the USA
- a description of the chef in his job
- where Glenn is at the moment

3 Match the American English expressions with their British English equivalents.

AMERICAN ENGLISH	BRITISH ENGLISH
standing in line	holiday
guess	Hello!
movie	queuing
mad	think
vacation	film
Hi!	angry

4 About you

1 Have you ever worked in a restaurant or hotel? What was it like?
2 What sort of temporary jobs can foreigners get in your country? What sort of permit do they need?

VOCABULARY

1 The verb to get

The verb *to get* has many different meanings e.g.
*to receive, to obtain,
to arrive (at).*
When used with an adjective it means *to become:*
*I'm getting tired. =
I'm becoming tired.*

When used with a past participle, it can have a passive meaning:
*I got fired. =
I was fired.* (passive)
Get occurs mostly in informal English.

Complete the sentences below. Make sure the tense of the verb *get* is correct.

GET + PARTICIPLE	GET + ADJECTIVE
get fired	get tired
get drunk	get angry
get lost	get ready
get married	get better

1 Ann has been very ill but at last she's . . .
2 Barry and Amy have just announced that they're going to . . .
3 The reason they were late was because they . . .
4 I made a lot of spelling mistakes because I . . .
5 When she can't find a parking space, she always . . .
6 If you're late again, you'll . . .
7 They're coming in ten minutes. Please hurry up and . . .
8 Have a good time at the party but don't . . .

2 There are several different ways of pronouncing *ea* in English. Look at the list below.

GROUP 1
/ɪː/ eat

GROUP 2
/e/ breakfast

GROUP 3
/eɪ/ break

GROUP 4
/ɪə/ ear

3 🔊 Listen and write the following words in the correct sound group.

tea   real   year   speak
theatre   (to) read   dead
mean   dear   ready
steak   pleased   head
leave   Shakespeare

🔊 LISTENING

An American student has just visited Stratford.

Note:
1 why she's in Britain.
2 what she thinks of the British theatre.
3 her impressions of Stratford.

TALKING POINT

List three arguments for or against living in places like Stratford-upon-Avon. In groups, discuss your arguments using the phrases below.

A: *The worst thing must be . . .*
A big disadvantage must be . . .
And what about the . . .
B: *Yes, but think of . . .*
An advantage must be . . .

22

Grammar

Present perfect simple and continuous

What's the difference in meaning?

1 He's worked in Stratford.   2 He's been working in Stratford.

Which verb tense is used in each sentence? Look back at the text about Glenn in Unit 21
Find all the examples of these two tenses. Check the Focus section below to see the
different ways in which the two tenses can be used.

FOCUS

The present perfect simple

This tense relates past events to present time.
It is used

- to talk about experiences and events at an
  unspecified time in the past:
  I've seen two plays by Shakespeare.
  I've never been to Stratford.

- to talk about something that is unfinished:
  I've lived in Stratford for ten years.

- to talk about events in a period of time that
  is not yet finished, e.g. _this morning/week:_
  I've been to two parties this week.

- to talk about a present result of a past
  event:
  _She's had an accident. She's broken
  her leg._

Note that it is often used in connection with
certain words:

- the time prepositions _since_ and _for:_
  She's lived here for three years.
  He's worked here since 1985.

- the adverbs _just_ and _already:_
  I've just finished it.
  I've already done it.
  These adverbs are not generally used in
  negative sentences with the present
  perfect.

- the adverb _yet_
  Have you done it yet?
  I haven't done it yet.
  This adverb is not used in positive
  sentences with the present perfect.

The present perfect continuous

This tense is used

- to describe an action which began in the
  past and is either still going on, or has
  recently stopped. Compare:

  I've been writing letters all morning.
  (Present perfect continuous. The activity
  is important.)
  I've written three letters. (Present perfect
  simple. The letters are now finished.)

- It is often used with _for_ and _since:_
  _I've been living here for a few months/
  since September._ (I am still living there.)

In which position in the sentence do the
adverbs _just, already_ and _yet_ occur in the
examples?

Identify the tenses in the short conversations
below.

A: What did you do last night?
B: I read a book.

A: Why are your eyes sore?
B: I've been reading.

A: Do you want to borrow this book?
B: No thanks, I've read it.

PRACTICE

1 Ask and answer about personal experiences, using the present perfect and the past simple of the verbs in the phrases below.

EXAMPLE

A: Have you ever been to the USA?
B: No, I haven't. Have you?
A: Yes, I went there with my parents two years ago.

1 go to the USA
2 break an arm or leg
3 see a famous person in real life
4 write to a magazine or newspaper
5 win a competition
6 find anything valuable

2 Look at the pictures. Ask and answer questions using the present perfect continuous.

EXAMPLE

1 A: What have you been reading?
  B: I've been reading a romantic novel.

1 What? 2 What? 3 What? 4 What? 5 Who?

3 In pairs, ask and say how long you have been doing the things in the list below. Use *for* or *since* in your answers.

1 living in your present home
2 studying in this school or college
3 learning English
4 using this textbook
5 doing this unit

4 Tell your partner about the following:

1 a sport or activity you've been doing a lot of recently
2 a sport you haven't done for a long time
3 a book you've been reading
4 a country you've always wanted to visit

🖭 LISTENING

Lori has written a letter to Glenn from Long Island in the USA and spoken it onto a cassette. Listen to her letter-cassette and say:

what annual event has just taken place.
what the weather's been like.
what happened to their summer cabin.
what she's been doing recently.

WRITING

Before you write

Look at the expressions below. You are writing an informal letter. Which would you use to: 1) start the letter 2) introduce a new topic 3) close the letter?

By the way, . . .
Did you know that . . .?
Thanks very much for your last letter.
Well, that's enough for now.
Sorry I haven't written before but . . .

It was great to get your letter.
Give my regards/love to . . .
Anyway, I'd better stop now.
Have you heard . . .?
Best wishes, . . .
Say hello to . . .
Love from . . .

Write a letter

Write to an English-speaking penfriend. Start by apologising for not writing before and give a reason. Describe some of the things you have done or have been doing recently. Say what the weather has been like. Close the letter by sending greetings to any other people you know.

-23-

Communication

Making complaints

Before you read

1 What do you think the woman is complaining about in the picture above?
2 What sort of things do people complain about in restaurants?
3 Have you ever complained in a restaurant? What about?

📼 DIALOGUE

WOMAN: How strange! This coffee is almost cold.
MAN: Yes, mine's not very hot either.
WOMAN: I'll call the waiter ... Excuse me!
WAITER: Yes?
WOMAN: I'm afraid this coffee isn't very hot. Could you bring us a fresh pot?
WAITER: Certainly. I'm sorry about that. We've got a problem in the kitchen. We're really rushed off our feet today. I'll get you some more straightaway.
WOMAN: Thanks very much.
(*Later*)
MAN: Excuse me.
WAITER: Yes, is anything the matter?
MAN: I'm sorry but I think you've charged us too much for the drinks. We only had one bottle of mineral water, not two. Would you mind checking the bill again?
WAITER: Let me see. Oh, right. I'm very sorry. I'll alter it immediately.
MAN: Thank you.
WOMAN: Well, apart from the coffee, that was a great meal.
WAITER: (*returning*) There you are. I've had a word with the manager and we haven't charged you for the coffee.
MAN: Oh, great! Thanks very much.

Listen and answer the questions.

1 What does the woman ask the waiter to do? Why?
2 What is the waiter's excuse?
3 What does the man ask the waiter to do? Why?
4 How does the restaurant offer to make amends?

FOCUS

Complaints/requests

● Making complaints:
  I'm afraid this coffee isn't very hot.
  I'm sorry but I think you've charged us too much for the drinks.
● Requesting action:
  Could you bring us a fresh pot?
  Would you mind checking the bill again?
  I'd be grateful if you could check the bill again.

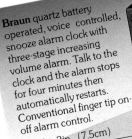

PRACTICE

1 Sort the words and phrases below into groups according to complaints about: automatic vending machines, hotel rooms, clothes and restaurant food.

doesn't work	zip broken
noisy	underdone
small	button missing
salty	gone wrong
dark	sweater shrunk
lining torn	broken down
cold	doesn't return
damp	coin
	overdone

Now use the words and phrases to practise making complaints.

2 In pairs, use the following situations to act out conversations.

1 You are in a restaurant and your hamburger is dry and overdone. You want the waitress to bring you another one.

2 You are in a hotel. Your room overlooks the rear car park and it is very noisy. Ask the receptionist to give you a different room.

3 You recently bought a pair of jeans but the first time that you wore them the zip broke. You take the jeans back to the shop to complain and ask for another pair in exchange.

4 You have put 50p into the automatic drinks machine to get a soft drink. The machine doesn't work and you have lost your 50p. You complain to one of the attendants and ask for your money back.

🎧 LISTENING

Listen to the telephone conversations. Note what the callers are complaining about and what action they are requesting.

READING

1 Read the two advertisements.

Find out:
what two products are advertised.
which one is waterproof.
which one responds to your voice.
how much the products cost.

2 Read the letter of complaint below to a mail order company.

Find out which product the customer bought, what is wrong with it and what the customer wants the company to do.

WRITING

You ordered a radio cassette player from the mail order company and it arrived last week. It worked well until you went on holiday. Now the fast forward button doesn't work when you press it. Write a letter of complaint.

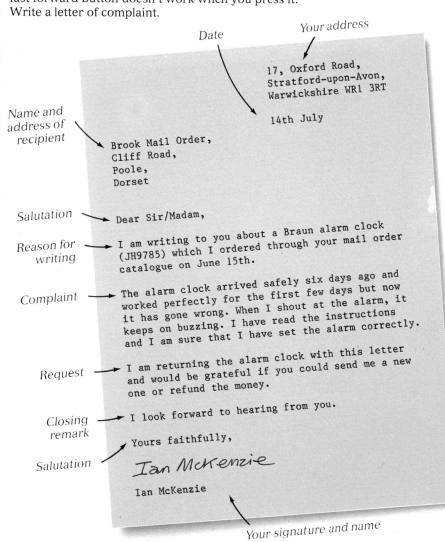

Date
Your address

17, Oxford Road,
Stratford-upon-Avon,
Warwickshire WR1 3RT

14th July

Name and address of recipient

Brook Mail Order,
Cliff Road,
Poole,
Dorset

Salutation → Dear Sir/Madam,

Reason for writing → I am writing to you about a Braun alarm clock (JH9785) which I ordered through your mail order catalogue on June 15th.

Complaint → The alarm clock arrived safely six days ago and worked perfectly for the first few days but now it has gone wrong. When I shout at the alarm, it keeps on buzzing. I have read the instructions and I am sure that I have set the alarm correctly.

Request → I am returning the alarm clock with this letter and would be grateful if you could send me a new one or refund the money.

Closing remark → I look forward to hearing from you.

Salutation → Yours faithfully,

Ian McKenzie

Ian McKenzie

Your signature and name

63

-24-

Grammar

Make and *do*

'I made a mistake with the breakfast orders.'

'Mr Partridge does the cooking.'

FOCUS

The verbs 'make' and 'do'
As you will see if you look in a dictionary, there are many uses of the verbs *make* and *do*. Here are some of them:

Make

- to create, produce or construct something:
  He made a delicious cake.

- to cause to be or happen:
  He made himself king.
  She made him angry.

- to force somebody to do something:
  She made him do his homework again.

Do

- to perform certain tasks and activities:
  He did his homework.
  I did the cleaning/ housework/shopping/ ironing/cooking.

- to perform actions which bring about a desired result:
  She's doing her hair/nails/ room.

- to talk about progress:
  How is she doing at school?

Note
There are also certain fixed phrases with *make* and *do*:

Make
a mistake   your bed   sure (that)   an effort   a noise
an arrangement   money/love/war   your mind up

Do
your best   business   research   your duty   a deal
a degree/course   (someone) a favour   some work

Look in your dictionary and find two more fixed phrases with *make* and *do* to add to the list.

PRACTICE

1 Rewrite these sentences using an expression with *make*.

1 I've decided to leave my job.
2 They fixed a time to meet.
3 I'd like you to try hard to arrive on time in future.
4 You've done something wrong here.
5 You can't force me to go.
6 He earned a lot of money buying and selling houses.

2 Rewrite these sentences using *do*.

1 It only takes me a second to tidy my room.
2 She is coming on very well at art school.
3 We buy everything we need in the new supermarket.
4 Last year he was trading with Russia.

3 Write sentences using *make* or *do*.

Describe the following:

1 a job in the home you like doing.
2 a job in the home you hate doing.
3 something you like cooking.
4 something you have made for yourself or your home.
5 an arrangement or promise you have recently made.
6 when and where you are going to do your homework.

4 Compare your list with your partner's.

-25-

Reading

Before you read

1 What famous plays do you know by Shakespeare?
2 Have you ever seen a Shakespeare play or a film of one of his plays?
3 In pairs, draw a plan of a theatre and label the following parts. Use a dictionary if necessary.

stage   curtain   footlights   actor   audience
stalls   circle   box   foyer   orchestra pit
aisle   exits

Guess the meaning

grandly   portrait   conspirator   dagger   offstage
walk-on   undermine   receive   distraction
commentary   curtain call   bow (v)   privilege

COMPREHENSION

1 Rearrange the eight paragraphs on the right to make four separate anecdotes about the theatre. The first paragraph is the start of the first anecdote but the rest are jumbled.

2 Match the headings below to the appropriate anecdote.

1 Joint performance
2 Hamlet made simple
3 Not known in Denver
4 A timely interruption

3 Summarise each anecdote using the prompts below.

1 This is about a very rich man who got angry when …
2 This is about an amusing incident during a performance of *Julius Caesar* when …
3 This is about an unusual performance of *Hamlet* when the actor in the title role …
4 This is about the famous actor, John Barrymore, whose performance of Hamlet was disturbed one afternoon by …

VOCABULARY

Which word does not belong in each group?
1 producer painter director actor
2 scene act (n) play box-office
3 chapter musical tragedy comedy
4 stalls box circle programme
5 orchestra footlights curtains spotlights

Theatrical anecdotes

a In 1881 a new opera house was built in Denver, Colorado, by the mining millionaire, H.A.W. Tabor. An English theatre company had been invited for the opening of the Tabor Grand. All of Denver society was there to see Mr Tabor, who was walking grandly about in the foyer. Suddenly he came upon a portrait of some unfamiliar person.

b His performance on the first night had not been greeted with much enthusiasm. This so undermined Cubit's confidence that he was taken ill on the second night just before curtain-up. The manager had to ask the audience to 'suffer a production' which omitted Hamlet entirely. It seems that the play was better received than on its first night, and many of the audience felt that it was an improvement on the complete play.

c John Barrymore did not seem to notice the star until his curtain call, when he bowed deeply towards her box and said: 'I'd like to take this opportunity to thank Miss Cowl for the privilege of co-starring with her this afternoon.'

d During a production of Shakespeare's *Julius Caesar*, two of the conspirators were about to murder Caesar. Their daggers were at the ready when the stage manager's phone rang just offstage.

e 'Who the hell is this?' he asked the person next to him.
'That's Shakespeare, Mr Tabor.'
'Who?'
'Shakespeare.'
'Who is Shakespeare?'
'He is the greatest playwright who ever lived.'
By this time, Tabor's face was turning dangerous colours of purple and red.
'I don't care,' the millionaire exploded. 'What the hell has he ever done for Colorado!?'
By next evening Shakespeare's portrait had been replaced by that of Mr Tabor.

f It was heard throughout the theatre. So was the remark of one of the conspirators to the other:
'What shall we do if it is for Caesar?'

g There have been very few occasions when a Shakespeare play has been performed in public without its main character. One such occasion was in 1787 when *Hamlet* was performed with no one in its title role. At the time the role was going to be played at the Richmond Theatre by an inexperienced actor called Cubit who had previously been given only small walk-on parts.

h During a performance of John Barrymore's *Hamlet* on Broadway, the film star Jane Cowl came to a matinée performance. Her presence caused a great distraction for the audience. She made matters worse by conducting a loud running commentary with her friends during the entire play.

–26–

Grammar

The passive

What's the difference in style?

1 They're building a new office block near our school.
2 An office block is being built near our school.

Which sentence is in the active and which is in the passive voice? Which sounds like something you would write in a report or a letter to a newspaper and which sounds like something you would say to a friend?

FOCUS

The passive

The passive is formed by combining the verb *to be* (in the tense required) with the past participle of the main verb.

Present simple:	is	
Present continuous:	is being	
Future:	will be	
Future *going to*: The musical	is going to be	performed . . .
Past simple:	was	
Past continuous:	was being	
Present perfect:	has been	
Past perfect:	had been	

The passive is used

- to give factual information:
  The musical Cats is based on the poems of T.S. Eliot.
  It was composed by Andrew Lloyd Webber.

- when what is/was done is more important than who is doing/did the action:
  Wine from California is exported to France.

- to introduce general opinions:
  It is now recognised as one of the most successful musicals of all time.

- to express rules:
  Smoking is not allowed here.
  It is forbidden to walk on the grass.

- to describe processes:
  Bread is made from flour.

Note
In daily, informal language we tend to use the active voice. The passive voice is used more often in formal written English.

Look at the text about 'Cats' above and notice the tense of each of the verbs in the passive voice.

CATS

The musical 'Cats', which is based on the poems of T.S. Eliot, was composed by Andrew Lloyd Webber and directed by Trevor Nunn. It was first produced in London in 1981 and has been performed in over nineteen capital cities of the world, including Budapest, Tokyo and of course New York. It is now recognised as one of the most successful musicals of all time.

PRACTICE

1 Using a passive each time, give an example of where they grow, produce or make each of the items below.

EXAMPLE
Wine is produced in many parts of France.
VW cars are made in Germany.

wine	tea	vodka
oil	coffee	(Name) cars
rice	bananas	whisky

2 In pairs, ask and say where in your country they do the following:

1 grow wheat, rice or potatoes
2 rear cattle
3 manufacture leather goods
4 mine coal or other minerals
5 catch a lot of fish
6 grow other fruit and vegetables

EXAMPLE
A: Where is wheat grown in (name of country)?
B: It's grown in (name of region or area), I think.

3 Complete the sentences with the present simple or past simple passive. Then say if the statements are true or false, and correct those that are false.

EXAMPLE

1 The 'Penny Black', the world's first postage stamp, was issued on May 6th, 1840. (True)

Check your answers with your teacher.

DID YOU KNOW?

1 The 'Penny Black', the world's first postage stamp, (issue) on May 6th, 1840.

2 The Volkswagen Beetle (design) in the early 1930s by Ferdinand Porsche, who better (know) for his typewriters.

3 A crude form of the ballpoint pen (invent) in 1888. Much later, in the 1930s, the ballpoint pen (make) famous by two Hungarian brothers by the name 'Biro'.

4 In one year, over 440 litres of soft drinks (drink) by one person in the USA.

5 Abraham Lincoln (assassinate) while having a meal in a restaurant.

6 The sound of a humming bird (produce) in its throat.

4 Say what is happening in the pictures using the present continuous passive.

EXAMPLE

1 The lions are being fed (by the lion keeper).

1 (feed)

4 (perform)

2 (chase)

5 (tell off)

3 (pick)

6 (demolish)

5 Read the politician's speech and convert his promises into a written manifesto using the future passive.

'By the end of next year I promise that we will reduce taxes and bring public spending under control. We will introduce wide-ranging educational reforms. What is more, we will keep our promise to increase teachers' salaries.

And I can assure you too, that we will not destroy the National Health Service, nor will we abandon our plans to improve inner city schools.

I've said it before, and I'll say it again. Nothing will stop us from fulfilling our promises.'

EXAMPLE

Manifesto

By the end of next year
- Taxes will be reduced.
- Public spending …

6 Discuss your personal experiences using the present perfect passive and the past simple passive of the verbs in the phrases.

EXAMPLE

A: Have you ever been stopped by the police?
B: No, I haven't but my brother has.
A: Really? Why?
B: He was stopped for speeding on the motorway.

1 stop by the police
2 interview on television
3 give a surprise party
4 fine for parking
5 search by customs
6 ask to give a speech
7 involve in a road accident

🔲 LISTENING

Listen to someone describing an audition. Note:

1 what the audition was for.
2 what character he was usually cast as.
3 what part he thought he was auditioning for.
4 what he was told to prepare.
5 how the audition went.
6 if he was chosen for the part.

WRITING

Use your notes from the Listening exercise to write a letter from the man to a friend.

Start like this:

Dear …

Did I tell you in my last letter that I was going to be auditioned for …? Well, the audition was …

27

Topic

The USA

Before you read

1 What do you know about New York City?
2 Where is it situated?
3 What are some of its famous sights?
4 Have you ever been there? What impressed you most?

THE EMPIRE STATE BUILDING

NEW YORK CITY is situated at the mouth of the Hudson River on the East coast of the USA. It is made up of five boroughs with a combined population of over 17 million people. The heart of New York City is the island of Manhattan, where, in the Midtown and Downtown districts, the buildings 'scrape the sky'.

One of these skyscrapers is the Empire State Building on Fifth Avenue, between 33rd and 34th Street. Like the Statue of Liberty and Brooklyn Bridge, it is instantly recognised as a symbol of New York — a symbol which captures the power, energy and excitement of one of the world's most-loved and most-hated cities.

When the 102-storey stucture was built in 1931, it was the tallest building in the world. From the top, on a clear day, you can see over a 50-mile radius. Its towering height and distinctive Art Deco style made the Empire State Building an instant success with the public.

Its record as the world's tallest building has since been beaten — the World Trade Center in New York and the Sears Tower in Chicago are both taller — but the Empire State Building remains uniquely fascinating.

At night it is floodlit with coloured lights. Some people love the lights but others complain that their favourite New York building has been turned into the biggest Christmas tree in the world!

EMPIRE STATE FACTS

★ The Empire State is 'stepped' above a certain height, rather like a pyramid, to prevent it from blocking light and air from the neighbouring area.

★ There are 6,500 windows, nearly seven miles of elevator shafts and enough floor space to shelter a town of 80,000 people.

★ The building was first cleaned in 1962. It took thirty people six months to complete the job. They were all experienced at high altitudes, including one who was a former paratrooper.

★ In the famous film 'King Kong', the giant gorilla, King Kong, has his final battle from the top of the Empire State.

Words to learn

district   scrape   instantly   symbol
power   energy   floodlit   prevent

1 Read and answer.

1 How many boroughs make up
New York City?
2 Where exactly is the Empire State Building
situated in Manhattan?
3 When was it built?
4 What happens to the building at night?
5 What happened in 1962?
6 Who was King Kong?

2 Correct the statements.

EXAMPLE
1 New York State is situated at the mouth of
the Mississippi River.
No, New York State is situated at the mouth
of the Hudson River.

2 In the downtown district of Manhattan the
buildings are small and old-fashioned.
3 The Empire State Building is the tallest
building in New York.
4 The Empire State was built in 1941.
5 It has never been cleaned.
6 The building is shaped like a tall rectangle.

3 About you

1 Have you ever been to the top of a high
building? Did you feel faint or giddy?
2 Does any building or monument in your
country fascinate you?
3 Can you name a place or building which is a
symbol of your country?

VOCABULARY

Types of buildings

1 Sort the following into order of:

Height
a) block of flats   c) house
b) skyscraper   d) bungalow

Size
a) detached house   c) palace
b) cottage   d) hut

Privacy
a) semi-detached house
b) terraced house
c) detached house
d) one-bedroom flat

2 Which is the odd word out?

a) warehouse   b) factory   c) villa
d) office block

▣ LISTENING

Listen to a woman talking about how her
original ideas about Americans and New York
in particular were altered by her visit. Copy and
complete the notes below as you listen.

	What she thought before	What she discovered
Americans in general personality topic of conversation		
New York The city 1 2 3 4 New Yorkers' clothes		

TALKING POINT

Discuss briefly how much influence you think
the following have had on the rest of the world.
Do you approve or disapprove of the influence?
– American films
– American film stars and personalities
– American food
– American music
– American clothes
– American politics

WRITING

Write a description of a famous building,
monument or landmark in your country.
PARAGRAPH 1
Say what the building is and where it is
situated. Say when it was built and who it was
designed by.
PARAGRAPH 2
Describe the building and any distinctive
features.
PARAGRAPH 3
Give any other information about the building
which makes it famous.

*A very famous building in . . . is . . ., situated
in/on . . . It was built in . . . and was designed by
the famous architect, . . .*

   *One of its main attractions is . . . It is/was
here that . . .*

28

Communication

Obligation and prohibition

FOCUS

Obligation and prohibition

- Ask about obligation:
  Do I have to wear an evening dress?
  Am I expected to wear an evening dress?
  Are we supposed to take a bottle?
  Do you think we should take a bottle?

- Talk about obligation:
  I think we should take a present with us.
  I think you're expected to dress up a bit.
  You're supposed to wear something smart.

- Talk about prohibition:
  You're not supposed to wear jeans.
  You mustn't/shouldn't have bare arms.

PRACTICE

1 In pairs, ask and say what you think you should do in the following social situations.

EXAMPLE

1 A teacher/class friend is leaving after a long time.
   A: What do you think we should do about Mrs Webster?
   B: I think we should collect some money for a present.

2 An elderly friend of the family is in hospital.
3 You are invited to a friend's wedding.
4 You are asked to lunch at your friend's parents' house.
5 A friend of the family dies.
6 You are inviting a Hindu family to a meal.

2 In pairs, complete the questionnaire below about polite behaviour in your country.

EXAMPLE

A: Do men have to wear jackets and ties in restaurants?
B: It depends on the restaurant. You don't have to in most restaurants but you're expected to wear a jacket and tie in expensive places.

3 Compare your answers with other pairs'.

Etiquette

A questionnaire

About clothing

1 Do men have to wear jackets and ties in restaurants?
2 Are men and women allowed to wear shorts to work in offices in summer?
3 Are there any special rules about what you have to wear in holy places?

About money

4 Is it rude to ask people how much money they earn?
5 Is a woman expected to pay her share of the bill in a restaurant?

About hospitality

6 Should you take a present when you are invited to somebody's home?
7 Is it rude to smoke without asking in other people's homes?
8 Is it impolite to smoke between courses?

About tipping

9 How much should you tip a taxi driver?
10 Is it the same in a restaurant and at the hairdresser's?

ABOUT BRITAIN

Table manners

Although rules regarding table manners are not very strict in Britain, it is considered rude to eat and drink noisily. At formal meals, the cutlery is placed in the order in which it will be used, starting from the outside and working in. The dessert spoon and fork are usually laid at the top of your place setting, not at the side.

After each course, the knife and fork should be laid side by side in the middle of the plate. This shows that you have finished and the plate can be removed. If you leave the knife and fork apart, it will show that you have not yet finished eating.

It is considered impolite to smoke between courses unless your hosts say otherwise. It is polite to ask permission before you smoke in people's homes.

In Britain, smoking is now forbidden in many public places, e.g. on the underground, on stations, in shops, in theatres and in cinemas.

📟 LISTENING

Listen to an American explaining American etiquette on table manners. Answer the following questions.
1 What is a man supposed to do before sitting down at the dinner table?
2 In which hand do Americans hold their fork?
3 When do they use their knife?
4 Where do they place the knife afterwards?

WRITING

Look at the example below, then write a few paragraphs about etiquette for visitors to your country. Give helpful advice about things like table manners, hospitality and tipping.

TALKING POINT

Discuss which of the following habits you consider rude and why.
Which of them, if any, do you consider acceptable only at home, and
which do you consider completely unacceptable?

– helping yourself to food without asking
– starting to eat before everyone is served
– picking at food with your hands
– reading at the meal table
– resting your elbows on the table
– reaching across the table in front of people
– leaving the table before other people have finished
– not thanking the cook
– wiping your plate clean with bread

ACT IT OUT

You are on a trip to Britain and you have been invited to dinner with a British family. In pairs or groups, act out the conversation when you ask your teacher before the event what you are supposed to do. Ask about clothes, forms of address, times to arrive and leave, gifts to take and how to thank your hosts.

Table Manners

At mealtimes in Sweden we don't use side plates for bread. You're supposed to put your bread on the table beside your dinner plate. After a meal, you're expected to thank the person who prepared it, even if it's your mother or father.

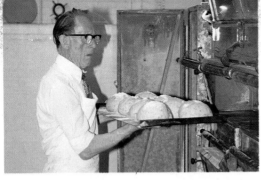

29

This is a baker who gave me some fresh bread when I was hungry.

The dog which followed me all over the Lake District.

These are some fishermen I met when I was in South Shields.

The man whose cauliflowers won first prize in the Flower Show.

Grammar

Defining relative pronouns

FOCUS

Defining relative clauses with 'who' 'which' 'that' 'where' and 'whose'.

1 *Who/that* **as a subject pronoun**

- These are used in defining relative clauses to define the person or people we are talking about:
  This is a baker who/that gave me some fresh bread.

2 *Which/that* **as subject pronouns**

- These are used in the same way to define things or places:
  This is the dog which/that followed me all over the Lake District.

3 *Who, which, that* **as object pronouns**

- When the person or thing is the object of the verb in the relative clause, you can leave out *who, which* or *that*:
  These are some fisherman (who/that) I met when I was in South Shields.

4 *Whose*

- *Whose* means *of whom* and replaces *his, her* and *their* in relative clauses. It can never be left out:
  That's the man whose cauliflowers won first prize in the flower show.

5 *Where*

- This means *in which* and is used to talk about places. It can never be left out.
  This is the village where I stayed in Devon.

Clovelly, the village where I stayed in Devon.

PRACTICE

1 Join the sentences with *who, whose, which* or *that*.

EXAMPLE

1 A man lent me his hammer. He lives next door.
The man who lives next door lent me his hammer.

2 A girl fainted. She was standing behind me in the queue. (The girl . . .)

3 Have you met the family? They have just moved in to the house next door. (Have you met . . .)

4 A man telephoned me this morning. His company sells computers.

5 What was the name of the car? It won the Car of the Year award.

2 Join the two sentences, omitting *who* or *which*.

EXAMPLE

1 That's the man. I was talking about him last night.
That's the man I was talking about last night.

2 Did you like the photo? I took it of you and your husband. (Did you . . .)

3 What did you do with the eggs? I bought them this morning. (What did . . .)

4 You spoke to a man on the phone. That was my father. (The man . . .)

5 They bought a house. It was very expensive. (The house . . .)

3 Match the phrases and the sentences below, then join them to make one sentence, using *where*.

EXAMPLE

1 That's the hotel . . .
That's the hotel where my sister spent her honeymoon.

2 Last night I went to a restaurant . . .
3 Over the road is the hairdresser's . . .
4 Why don't you go to the garage . . .
5 I went back to the part of the beach . . . but I couldn't find it.
6 That's the library . . .

A I usually have my hair cut there.
B My sister spent her honeymoon there.
C You can eat as much as you like for £10 there.
D I lost my watch there.
E They usually have interesting art exhibitions there.
F I take my car to be serviced there.

4 In pairs, ask about and identify the people in the picture. Use *who* or *whose* and choose from the character descriptions below.

EXAMPLE

A: Who's the woman in the red dress?
B: That's Ann. She's the one I told you about who overslept and missed the plane home.

ANN   She overslept and missed the plane home.
SALLY   Her bed broke in the middle of the night.
MARK   He stayed in his hotel room most of the day.
LUCY   She went out with one of the hotel waiters.
ROBERT His wallet was stolen on the beach.
JAN   Her hotel room caught fire.
GORDON His back got badly sunburnt.

WRITING

Write a paragraph describing in detail one of the items below. See how many relative clauses you can use.

– the last book you read
– a film you saw recently
– a supermarket where you usually do your shopping
– a town you like very much

How to be an alien

THE LANGUAGE

When I arrived in England I thought I knew English. After I'd been here an hour, I realised I did not understand a word.

THE WEATHER

You must never contradict anybody when discussing the weather. Should it hail and snow, should hurricanes uproot the trees from the side of the road, and should someone remark to you: 'Nice day, isn't it?' — answer without hesitation: 'Isn't it lovely!'

'Nice day, isn't it?'   'Isn't it lovely!'

QUEUEING

An Englishman, even if he is alone, forms an orderly queue of one. At weekends an Englishman queues up at the bus stop, travels out to Richmond, queues up for a boat, then queues up for tea, then queues up for ice cream, then joins a few more odd queues just for the fun of it, then queues up at the bus stop and has the time of his life.

PETS

If you go out for a walk with a friend, don't say a word for hours; if you go out for a walk with your dog, keep chatting to him.

HOW TO PLAN A TOWN

1 First of all, never build a street straight.
2 Give a different name to a street whenever it bends.
3 Call streets by various names: street, road, place, mews, crescent, avenue, lane, way, park, gardens, path, walk, broadway, promenade, gate, terrace, view, hill etc.

TEA

The trouble with tea is that originally it was quite a good drink. So a group of the most eminent British scientists put their heads together, and made complicated biological experiments to find ways of spoiling it.

They suggested that if you do not drink it clear but pour a few drops of cold milk into it, and no sugar at all, the desired object is achieved. Once this refreshing, aromatic, oriental beverage was successfully transformed into colourless and tasteless gargling water, it suddenly became the national drink of Great Britain and Ireland.

There are some occasions when you must not refuse a cup of tea. If you are invited to an English home, at five o'clock in the morning a cup of tea is brought in by a heartily smiling hostess. You have to declare with your best five o'clock smile: 'Thank you so much. I do adore a cup of early morning tea, especially early in the morning.' If you are left alone with the liquid, you may pour it down the washbasin.

Then you have tea for breakfast; then you have tea at eleven o'clock in the morning; then after lunch; then you have tea for tea; then after supper; and again at eleven o'clock at night.

How to be an alien was written by George Mikes (pronounced /mɪkeʃ/), a Hungarian who came to live in Britain. It was first published in 1946 and has since been reprinted over forty times.

George Mikes said his book was meant: 'chiefly for xenophobes (people who dislike foreigners) and anglophobes (people who dislike England and the English).' The extract on the left includes some of the observations which have delighted generations of readers.

Guess the meaning

alien   contradict
hurricane   eminent
complicated   experiment
spoil   refreshing
aromatic   transform   adore

COMPREHENSION

Read the text above and the extract on the left and answer the questions.

1 Where did George Mikes come from?
2 When was *How to be an alien* first published?
3 What sort of book is it?
4 What does George Mikes say about the English
  – language?
  – attitude to the weather?
  – habit of queueing?
  – attitude to pets?
  – towns?
  – way of serving tea?
  – tea-drinking habits?

> **Glossary**
> **Richmond** an attractive town on the river Thames
> **has the time of his life** has a marvellous time
> **beverage** drink
> **gargling liquid** liquid to wash inside the throat and mouth

VOCABULARY

Adjective formation with *-less* and *-ful*

The suffix *-less* means *without*, e.g. *colourless = without colour*.
The suffix *-ful* means *with*, e.g. *colourful = with colour*

1 Combine a noun from the box with *-less* to make adjectives which describe the definitions below.

heart	care	pain	shape	home	use	job	thought

EXAMPLE
1 people who have nowhere to live
   homeless

2 people who are cruel and unkind
3 people who are inattentive and don't take care
4 people who don't think about what they say or do
5 something which doesn't hurt
6 something that has no form
7 something that is broken or has no value
8 people who are out of work

Which of these adjectives can also be used as a noun to apply to people, in the same way as *the rich* and *the poor*?

2 Which of the nouns in Exercise 1 can be combined with *-ful* to make an adjective?

3 Sort the adjectives below into two groups to indicate a positive or a negative opinion.

true	silly	affectionate
funny	rude	xenophobic
stereotypical	superficial	old-fashioned
cruel	perceptive	witty

Which of them would you use to describe George Mikes's comments?

🔲 LISTENING

Before you listen

Read the dictionary entry for a definition of *stereotype*.

ster·e·o·type[1] /'steriətaɪp/ *n* [(**of**)] *usu. derog* (someone or something that represents) a fixed set of ideas about what a particular type of person or thing is like, which is (wrongly) believed to be true in all cases: *She believes that she is not a good mother because she does not fit the stereotype of a woman who spends all her time with her children.* | *The characters in the film are just stereotypes with no individuality.* | *racial stereotypes* —**-typical** / steriəʊˈtɪpɪkəl/ *adj*

Listen

Some people are discussing a joke based on national stereotypes of the Scots, the Irish and the English.

Note:
what national characteristics are implied in the joke.
how the Irishman felt about the joke.
what other types of joke the people thought were perhaps more offensive.

TALKING POINT

What are your views about the British? Make a note of your views on the following subjects:
– language
– attitude to work
– attitude to foreigners
– food
– dress sense
– homes
– behaviour/manners
– young people

How many of your views are positive, and how many are negative? Compare your opinions in groups. How many of your opinions are the same? Do you think this means they are stereotypes?

WRITING

Write paragraphs about national stereotypes. Say if you think they are true or not.

Many people think/say that the (name of nationality) are . . . . This is probably because . . . . In fact, ...

The (name of nationality) are said/thought to . . . because . . . but most of the people I know . . . .

Jokes are often made about us because we . . . and in some ways I think this is true.

A popular view of . . . is that we all . . . but actually . . . .

'And will you be going to Cruft's this year as usual, Florence?'

Check

1 Complete the parts of these irregular verbs.

EXAMPLE
break – broke – broken

1 break	5 bring	9 drive
2 fall	6 speak	10 see
3 spend	7 spill	11 give
4 steal	8 take	12 write

2 Write the correct form of the verbs in brackets, using the past simple or the present perfect simple tenses.

1 A: When (you/buy) the compact disc player?
 B: I (buy) it last week.
2 A: What (you/do) to your hair? It looks great.
 B: I (just/have) a haircut.
3 A: (You/ever/be) to America?
 B: Yes, I (go) there last year.
4 A: (You/see) my glasses? I can't find them.
 B: When (you/have) them last?
5 A: You must write and thank Aunt Julie for her present.
 B: I (already/write).
6 A: Oh no! I (spill) chocolate milkshake all down my jacket.
 B: I'll get a cloth.
7 A: (You/see) the new Spielberg film yet?
 B: Yes, I (see) it last night, in fact.
8 A: What (you/say) when you (speak) to Jeremy?
 B: I (not/speak) to him yet.

3 Complete the sentences with the correct form of the present perfect simple or continuous.

1 I can smell garlic. What (you/cook)?
2 She (already/smoke) a whole packet of cigarettes and it's only three o'clock!
3 (you/see) George? He was here a minute ago.
4 It looks as if I (cry), doesn't it? In fact, I (peel) onions.
5 Where (you/put) my magazine? I can't see it.
6 I still (not/finish) that book although I (read) it for weeks.
7 Didn't you hear me? I (knock) at the door for ages!
8 She's walking a bit strangely. Maybe she (hurt) herself.

4 Complete the conversation choosing from the sentences below.

YOU: (1) . . .?
GLENN: Oh travelling around Europe for a bit and doing odd jobs here and there.
YOU: (2) . . .?
GLENN: What? Here in Stratford? Oh, for a few days.
YOU: (3) . . .?
GLENN: Yes, I have. In a hotel.
YOU: (4) . . .?
GLENN: It's just a small one. You won't know it.
YOU: (5) . . .?
GLENN: Yes, I've seen 'Hamlet' and 'King Lear'.
YOU: (6) . . .?
GLENN: Yes, I did, especially 'Hamlet'.
YOU: (7) . . .?
GLENN: Yes, I've been to see Anne Hathaway's Cottage and Shakespeare's birthplace.
YOU: (8) . . .?
GLENN: Yes, I have. It's a great place, Stratford!

A: Have you been working?
B: Well you sound as if you've been enjoying yourself.
C: What have you been doing this summer?
D: Which hotel have you been working in?
E: Did you enjoy them?
F: And have you done any sightseeing?
G: How long have you been here?
H: Have you seen any Shakespeare plays yet?

5 Insert the correct form of *make* or *do* in the sentences.

1 Could you . . . me a cup of tea?
2 I haven't . . . my homework yet.
3 The business isn't . . . very well at the moment.
4 We would like everyone to . . . their beds every day and to . . . some cleaning.
5 Did you hear that they . . . her president of the club?
6 Try not to . . . a noise when you go upstairs.
7 I wish you would . . . up your mind about coming or not.
8 Could you . . . me a favour and shut the door?

6 Write the correct form of the verbs in brackets, using the passive.

1 A lot of apples (grow) in Normandy in France.
2 Meat (export) by Argentina to the rest of the world.
3 The forests of Northern Europe (destroy) slowly by acid rain.
4 'Hamlet' (write) by Shakespeare.
5 Do you know how President Abraham Lincoln (assassinate)?
6 The homework for the last lesson (not correct) yet.
7 Guess what! I (invite) to Jessica's party.

7 Choose the correct tense (the present simple passive or present continuous passive and then rewrite the sentences.

1 A: Waiter, is my food ready? I'm in a hurry.
  B: It won't be long, sir. It's *cooked/being cooked* at the moment.
2 A: Is this bag plastic or leather?
  B: Madam, it's *being made/made* of the finest Italian leather.
3 A: Where's your car?
  B: It's *being repaired/repaired*.
4 A: Why are the children *sent/being sent* to bed?
  B: Because they've been naughty.
5 A: How are you all getting home from the airport?
  B: We're *being met/met* by my father.

8 Complete the paragraph by inserting relative pronouns where necessary.

Aesop was a Greek writer . . . probably lived in the 6th century B.C. Little is known about his life. He wrote fables (short stories . . . teach a particular lesson). Most of the fables . . . he wrote are about animals . . . speak and act like people. A fable . . . most people have read is called 'The Hare and the Tortoise'.

9 Circle the odd vowel sound in these groups of words.

1 eat   feed   lean   dear
2 we're   here   where   fear
3 head   mean   instead   bed
4 where   wear   hair   ear
5 speak   break   weak   clean

10 Match the words and phrases in the left hand column with the opposite word in the right hand column.

1 noisy   a correct
2 small   b polite
3 salty   c kind
4 damp   d deep
5 broken   e quiet
6 overdue   f dull
7 wrong   g dry
8 in working order h sweet
9 cruel   i large
10 rude   j fixed
11 witty   k broken down
12 superficial   l underdone

11 Circle the best sentences.

1 A: Can I help you?
  B: a) I'm sorry the zip on this shirt is broken.
     b) Yes, I'm afraid the zip on this shirt is broken.
     c) This zip is breaking.
2 B: a) Would you mind changing it please?
     b) Do you mind if you change it please?
     c) Please change it.
  A: No, not at all.
3 A: The invitation looks very formal.
     a) Do you think I must wear a dress?
     b) Do you think I should wear a dress?
     c) Do I expect to wear a dress?
4 A: Do we really have to go to the wedding?
  B: a) Yes, I think we're allowed to go.
     b) Yes, we had to go.
     c) Yes, I think we're expected to go.

12 Rearrange the jumbled sentences below and write a letter of complaint. Start your letter with *Dear Sir/Madam,*.

1 Could you also let me know if you would like the stereo returned.
2 A month ago I ordered a personal stereo from your firm.
3 I look forward to hearing from you.
4 There are several marks on it and one of the buttons doesn't work.
5 When it arrived, I found that the stereo had been damaged in the post.
6 I would be grateful if you could replace it or give me a refund.

Use your English

1 In pairs, take turns to make conversations. Choose a suitable time expression each time from the list below.

I was nineteen   three weeks   a few months ago
1985   quite a while   last August
my eighteenth birthday   a couple of months
about eight years   January of last year

1 A: Where do you live?
   B: In the centre of Paris.
   A: How long …
   B: I've … since …

2 A: Is that a new sound system?
   B: Yes it is.
   A: How long …
   B: I've … for …

3 A: I didn't know you could drive!
   B: Yes, I can.
   A: How long …
   B: I've … since …

4 A: Your English is good.
   B: Thank you.
   A: How long …
   B: I've … for …

2 (Student B: page 127)
There are a number of missing words in your reading text (1, 3, 5, 7 and 9). Student B has the same text but with different missing words (2, 4, 6, 8 and 10). Complete your texts by asking each other in turn for the missing information, using the question word in brackets. You start.

EXAMPLE
A: (1) What was the man called?
B: He was called Sir Guy Fawkes.
B: (2) Who did he plot to blow up?
A: He …

Guy Fawkes Day
In 1606 in London, a man called … (1 What?) plotted to blow up King James I and the Houses of Parliament. The plot, called … (3 What?), was discovered on 4th November. Guy Fawkes and his friends were executed on … (5 When?). Since then, every 5th November, people let off fireworks, light … (7 What?) and burn a 'guy' – a life-size dummy which represents Guy Fawkes. Some people have bonfire parties … (9 Where?) but nowadays a public bonfire display is organised in most towns and villages.

3 (Student B: page 127)
You are an assistant in a department store. Student B is a customer with a number of complaints. Look at the pictures and ask what the matter is. Offer to change the item for another each time.

EXAMPLE
A: Is there anything wrong with your trousers?
B: Yes, I'm afraid the pocket is torn.
A: Oh, I'm sorry. I'll change them for another pair.

Now it is your turn to be the customer. This time you are in a restaurant. Look at the pictures below and tell Student B, the waiter, what is wrong each time.

4 In pairs, rearrange the sentences in the correct order to form a paragraph about tipping in restaurants in Britain.

a) service charge to their customers'
b) restaurant. However, many restaurants in
c) been bad, you do not have to pay it.
d) As a general rule, you are supposed
e) bill. This means that you are not
f) you are particularly pleased with
g) Britain today automatically add a 10%
h) the service. In fact, the service charge is not
i) expected to leave a tip on top of this unless
j) obligatory and if you think the service has
k) to leave a 10–12% tip in a

Start like this:

(d) As a general rule, you are supposed (k) to leave a 10–12% tip in a …

Progress test

GRAMMAR

1 Choose the correct answer.

1 … here since ten o'clock?

a) Are you   b) Were you   c) Have you been

2 What time … yesterday?

a) did you leave   b) have you left
c) were you leaving

3 How many times … her so far today?

a) did you phone   b) have you phoned
c) have you been phoning

4 It smells as if you … onions.

a) have been frying   b) have fried   c) fry

5 This house … a hundred years ago.

a) is built   b) was built   c) been built

6 When she makes a mistake, she always … angry.

a) is   b) is getting   c) gets

7 Do you think I … write or telephone?

a) should   b) ought   c) am expected

8 He's the man … car got stolen.

a) who   b) who's   c) whose

9 Don't disturb her. She's … her exercises.

a) making   b) taking   c) doing

10 Cars … in this country in large numbers.

a) is produced   b) are produce
c) are produced

2 Correct the sentences.

1 Did you find your tennis racket yet?
2 They've been married since three years.
3 Sorry I don't write before now.
4 I better stop now. It's getting late.
5 I'm afraid this hamburger it is overdone.
6 I am grateful if you could change it.
7 I did a bad mistake in that sentence.
8 The woman which lives next door lent me her
ladder.

VOCABULARY

3 Choose the correct word.

1 He got lost/fired from his job when they found
out what he had done.
2 The opposite of a permanent job is a short
time/temporary job.
3 Something that is worth a lot of money is very
valuable/worthy.
4 I'm afraid your sweater has shrunk/reduced in
the wash.
5 He managed to break/tear the sleeve of his jacket
when he climbed over the wall.
6 She rang to say that her car had broken up/
broken down.
7 I wonder if you could do me a kindness/favour?
8 I've finally/after all decided where I'm going for
my holiday.
9 My parents have bought a little villa/cottage in
the country.
10 If you go to the hairdressers, it is polite to leave
a gratuity/tip.
11 The knife and fork should be laid side to side/
side by side on the plate.
12 It's rather dark. Would you like me to
accompany/follow you to the station?
13 When you are waiting for a bus in Britain, it is
important to form a queue/line.
14 It was very thoughtless/careless of you to lose
your passport.
15 'You're looking well,' she remarked/noticed.

USAGE

4 Complete each of the numbered gaps in the text from the list below.

dealing   which   interviews   is   shake   cause
thing   good   made   who   about   in

**Janet Payne from EMI Records talks about the
sort of people she likes to employ.**
'There are particular types of people …(1)… fit into
the record industry; they are usually outgoing,
positive and …(2)… communicators. I am interested
…(3)… the way they come forward to …(4)… hands and
the way in which they talk …(5)… themselves. In jobs
where they are going to be …(6)… with artists,
somebody who mumbles or …(7)… vastly
overconfident can have a negative effect and …(8)…
problems. Clothes don't matter at all. The only
…(9)… I don't like is people who have obviously
…(10)… no effort. We have people turning up for
…(11)… in jeans, leggings and shorts, all of …(12)… are
fine.'

LOCAL CRAFT IS ALIVE AND WELL

Eve

A jewellery maker

John Marsham meets Eve Maxwell, a 26-year-old jewellery maker from Avebury in Wiltshire

I FIRST MET Eve Maxwell in a covered market in Bath, where she has a stall. As we chatted, some people gathered, fingering the silver necklaces, bracelets and earrings on display. Eve had her eye constantly on the stall. 'If you turn your back for a moment, you can lose the lot.'

I asked her if she worked only in silver. 'Yes, silver fascinates me. I like the feel and look of it.' Eve makes her jewellery in a small cottage in Avebury, a village set in the high chalk downs of North Wiltshire. We drove back there after the market closed. 'I first came here when I was a student at art school. We had to do some sketches of the prehistoric stones. I fell in love with the place immediately. It's so peaceful. I'd go mad if I had to live in London.'

'Another good reason for living here is financial. If I had a market stall in London, in Portobello Road for example, I'd have to pay an enormous rent and it would cut my profits considerably.

'You have to be quite tough to set up your own business, particularly as a jeweller. Some stall holders are quite unscrupulous, especially in the antique side of the business. They don't put price tags on anything and they charge what they like if they think a customer will pay it. I couldn't do that. If I were a man, I'd probably be more aggressive about selling, but I do well enough. I also take commissions from people who want something special designed and made.

'My parents would prefer me to get a full-time job but I'd lose my independence if I did that. I enjoy being my own boss. I may not make a fortune but at least I can choose the hours I work. Besides, I love the creative part of the work. I would hate to work in an office all day.'

Words to learn
constantly   fascinate
financial   tough
unscrupulous   aggressive
independence

1 Read and answer.

1 Where did the reporter first meet Eve?
2 What sort of jewellery does Eve sell?
3 Where does she live?
4 When did she first visit Avebury? Why?
5 What are Eve's reasons for not living in London?
6 Apart from selling jewellery on the stall, how else does she make money?
7 Why does she like her job?

Glossary
Wiltshire a county (an administrative district) in south-west England
chalk downs rounded hills of chalk
Portobello Road a street market specialising in antiques, jewellery and clothes

2 Read and think.

1 Why do you think that Eve 'had her eye constantly on the stall'?
2 Why do you have to be tough to set up your own business?
3 What is wrong with not having price tags?
4 What impression do you get of Eve?

3 About you

1 Are there any interesting markets you go to? What special things can you buy there?
2 Would you like to go into business on your own? Why/why not?

4 Read about Britain

What's special about Bath?

ABOUT BRITAIN

Bath

Bath was, and still is, the most famous spa in England. It is the only resort with natural hot springs (49°C / 120°F) and is one of England's most beautiful towns. In the first century AD the Romans built elaborate baths at the hot springs. Today the Roman baths and the elegant Georgian architecture with its well-proportioned facades are strong tourist attractions.

VOCABULARY

1 Find words or expressions from the text about Eve which have the same meaning as the following:

talk informally   all the time   drawings
related to money   hard (of people)   dishonest

2 Where do you wear the following?

EXAMPLE
1 You wear earrings on/in your ears.

1 earrings	4 brooch	7 ring
2 cuff-links	5 bracelet	8 gold chain
3 necklace	6 pendant	9 watch

3 In pairs, describe any jewellery you are wearing. Do you have a favourite piece of jewellery? If so, what is it?

4 Use a dictionary to find out how the following words are pronounced and write them in sound groups, e.g. *tough* /tʌf/.

though	brought	thought
bought	cough	although
nought	enough	ought
rough	fought	through

5 ▣ Now listen to the tape and see if you were right.

▣ LISTENING
Before you listen

Look these words up in a dictionary:

tweezers, file, pliers, pincers, scissors

Listen

Listen to Phil, a jewellery maker, talking about his job. Then listen again and each time you hear the bleep, note down the question which you think the interviewer asked.

TALKING POINT

1 What is most important for you in a job? Write the following in order of importance, and add any other aspects which are important to you.

travel	money
your colleagues	holidays
being your own boss	the hours
meeting people	chance of promotion
variety	job satisfaction
working conditions	perks (e.g. car, lunch)

2 In groups, talk about your list.

WRITING
Linking devices: listing reasons

Choose a job which you would like to do and write a paragraph about the reasons why you would like to do it. Use the linking devices below to help you.

EXAMPLE
The main reason for wanting/choosing to be a travel courier is because it's a way of seeing the world. *Another good reason* is that you get a chance to meet lots of different people. *Besides,* I enjoy travelling.

32

Grammar

Second conditional
if clauses

What's the difference in meaning?

1. I'll lose my independence if I get a full-time job.
2. I'd lose my independence if I got a full-time job.

What differences are there in the verb tenses between the two sentences? Which sentence is a 'first conditional' and which is a 'second conditional'?

Find more examples of the second conditional from the text about Eve. Are they all used in the same way? Check by looking at the Focus section below.

FOCUS

The second conditional

This structure is used

- to talk about hypothetical but possible situations:
  If I had a stall in London, I'd have to pay an enormous rent.

- to talk about totally imaginary or impossible situations:
  If I were a man, I'd probably be more aggressive.

- to give advice:
  If I were you, I'd get a full-time job.

Points to note

- *Would* never occurs in the *if* clause.

- The verb in the *if* clause is always in the past tense even though it refers to future or present time.

- *Were* is often used instead of *was* after *if*, especially in written English:
  If he were here, he'd . . .
  Was often occurs in informal spoken English.

PRACTICE

1 Discuss the following situations with your partner.

1 What would you do if you won £100? £1,000? £10,000?
2 Who would you like to be if you woke up tomorrow as a different person?
3 What three things would you take with you if you were shipwrecked on a desert island?
4 Which single item would you save if your house/flat caught fire?

EXAMPLE
A: What would you do if you won £100?
B: I think I'd buy . . ./invest it in . . ./spend it on . . ./give it to . . .

2 In pairs, imagine that one of you is a tourist visiting your town or city for the day. Practise asking for and giving the best advice in the following situations. Start your questions with:

Where/What can I . . .
What/How do you think I should . . .

EXAMPLE
A: Excuse me.
   Where can I buy a good map of the town?
B: If I were you, I'd go to . . .

You want to know:
1 where to buy a good map of the town.
2 what important sights to see.
3 the best way of getting around the tourist sights.
4 what local food dishes to try.
5 the best place to change money.

3 In pairs, ask and answer the questions to complete the questionnaire on the opposite page for your partner. Then check your scores to find out how assertive he/she is.

HOW ASSERTIVE ARE YOU?

What would you do in these situations?

Complete the questionnaire and check your scores.

	Yes	No
1 If someone lit up a cigarette in a non-smoking area, would you tell them to put it out?		
2 If someone parked their car in your parking space, would you ask them to move it?		
3 If you were in a shop and wanted change for a £10 note, would you buy something small first before asking for change?		
4 If you badly wanted a glass of water while you were in town, would you go into a restaurant and ask for it?		
5 If a group of friends wanted you to go out with them, would you do so, even if you felt too tired?		
6 If you were late for a flight, would you go to the front of the check-in queue without waiting your turn?		
7 If someone pushed in front of you in a queue at the bank, would you say something to them?		
8 If you bought a pair of shoes and the heels came loose after a week, would you take them back to the shop and complain?		
9 If you weren't enjoying a play at the theatre, would you stay until the end?		
10 If a good friend asked to borrow a large sum of money, would you lend it if you had it?		

SCORING

Questions 1,2,4,6,7,8 Yes = 2 points No = 0 points.
Questions 3,5,9,10 No = 2 points Yes = 0 points.

The higher your score, the more assertive you are.

Fourteen or over: You have a strong personality. You insist on other people respecting your rights. Some people may think you are 'pushy' and aggressive.

Eight or under: You have a submissive personality and like to follow rather than to lead. People often take advantage of your good nature.

ACT IT OUT

In pairs, act out what you would say if you were:
– the smoker and the non-smoker in (1).
– the two car drivers in (2).
– the manager of the shoe shop and the customer in (8).
– the two friends in (10).

TALKING POINT

If you knew you could devote your life to any single occupation – in music, writing, acting, business, politics, medicine, etc – and be among the best and most successful in the world at it, what would you choose and why?

🖭 LISTENING

Listen to some people discussing the same question. Which occupations did they choose? Did they give the same answers as you?

33

Communication

Polite requests for information

🔊 DIALOGUE

EVE: Hello. Can I speak to Dave Edgar please?

WOMAN: I'm afraid he isn't home from work yet. Who's speaking?

EVE: It's Eve Maxwell here, a friend of his. Have you any idea when he'll be back?

WOMAN: I'm not sure. He sometimes works late.

EVE: I see. Could you tell me what his work number is? I'm afraid I've lost it.

WOMAN: Yes, hold on while I look in the book. It's 31556.

EVE: Thanks. By the way, do you know if he received a parcel this morning?

WOMAN: No, I don't. I could go and ask my husband.

EVE: No, don't bother. I'm phoning from a public call box. Anyway, thanks for your help. Goodbye.

WOMAN: Goodbye.

Listen and answer the questions.

1 Who does Eve want to speak to?
2 Where is he?
3 Do you think the woman is Dave Edgar's
   a) wife b) landlady c) girlfriend?
4 What three things does Eve want to know?

FOCUS

- **Asking for information politely:**

  Could/Can you tell me what his work number is, please?
  Have you any idea when he'll be back?
  Do you know if he received a parcel this morning?

  Points to note
  - Polite requests for information are followed by an indirect question in the subordinate clause:
    Could/Can you tell me +what his work number is, please?
    The word order in the subordinate clause is always: subject + verb.

  - The subordinate clause can be introduced by a question word, e.g. *what/where/how,* or by *if:*
    Do you know where he is?
    Do you know if he received a parcel this morning?

  - If you have several questions to ask the same person, it is perfectly polite to start with an indirect question and continue with direct questions.

PRACTICE
Convert the following direct questions into indirect questions.

EXAMPLE
1 How far is it to Bath?
   Do you know how far it is to Bath?

2 Is there a hamburger restaurant here?
   Can you tell me . . .
3 Where's the nearest bank?
   Could you tell me . . .
4 What time does the market close?
   Have you any idea . . .
5 Where can I buy a phone card?
   Can you tell me . . .
6 Are there any buses which go from here to the station?
   Could you tell me . . .

ACT IT OUT
In pairs, act out three conversations.

Write down two consecutive questions you might want to ask in each of the following places: 1) a railway station 2) a post-office and 3) a sports stadium.

Then take turns to ask politely for information in each place. Make sure you start the conversation with an indirect question and give sensible replies to each question.

EXAMPLE
A: Excuse me, can you tell me what time the next train to Bath leaves?
B: Yes, it leaves at 10.15.

▣ LISTENING
Before you listen

Adrian Taylor is planning to sail singlehanded across the Atlantic. Think of six questions to ask him.

EXAMPLE
Why do you want to sail the Atlantic alone?

Listen

Note the questions which the interviewer asked Adrian Taylor. How many of the questions were the same as yours? Which of them were indirect questions?

True or false?

1 Adrian is doing the trip because a friend challenged him to do it.
2 He's been training hard.
3 So far he has received £80 in sponsorship.
4 He doesn't know exactly when he is going to leave.
5 He's hoping to complete the trip in less than a month.
6 His family are worried about the trip.

WRITING

Write a short newspaper article about Adrian Taylor and give it a suitable headline.

Start like this:

BON VOYAGE!
On Saturday, 15th June, Adrian Taylor, aged twenty-two, is leaving Portsmouth in an attempt to sail singlehanded across the Atlantic. To prepare for the crossing, Adrian has been . . .

Read about Britain

Find out how to use a phone card.

ABOUT BRITAIN

Phone cards

In many telephone booths in Britain you can use phone cards instead of money. These cards come in 10p units (20, 40, 100 or 200) and are on sale at post offices, newsagents and railway stations. To make a phone call you insert the card, dial the number and speak. As you talk, you can see on the digital display how many units you have left on the card.

34

Grammar

Have/Get something done

RED STAR GARAGE
Special Offer This Week!
With every £50 you spend:
FREE
tyres and oil check
car wax and polish
windscreen wash
battery check

🔲 DIALOGUE

MAN: You need some more brake fluid. That's why the warning light's on.

EVE: I'm having the car serviced on Friday. I'll get the brake fluid topped up then.

MAN: I think you ought to have it done straightaway. I'll do it for you now.

EVE: Fine. By the way, I'd like my tyres checked too, please.

MAN: Sure.

Listen and answer the questions.
1 Why is the warning light on?
2 What's happening on Friday?
3 What else would Eve like done?

What's the difference in meaning?
1 I'm servicing the car.
2 I'm having the car serviced.

FOCUS

Causative 'have' and 'get'

- To *have* or *get something done* means that you arrange for someone else to do a job; you do not do it yourself:
  I'm having/getting the car serviced on Friday.
  I think you ought to have/get it done straightaway.

- *I'd like it done* is a shorter and more usual way of saying: *I'd like to have it done.*

PRACTICE

1 In pairs, say what you are going to have done at the Red Star Garage.

EXAMPLE
I'm going to have my tyres checked.

Then ask for it to be done.

EXAMPLE
I'd like my tyres checked, please.

2 Define the following people and places.

a decorator   a plumber   a carpenter   a builder   an engineer
a garage   a cleaner   a tailor   a dressmaker

Say which of the following jobs you do yourself and which you have done by the people or the places above.

EXAMPLE

A: Do you do your own decorating?
B: It depends. I do small jobs myself but if it's a big job, I have it done by a painter and decorator.

A: Would you repair a leaking tap yourself?
B: No, I can't do things like that myself. I'd get/have it repaired by a plumber.

Do you . . .?

1 do your own decorating
2 alter or mend your own clothes
3 service your own car
4 clean your own home

Would you . . . yourself?

5 repair a leaking tap
6 repair/fix your TV
7 make some bookshelves
8 knock down or build a wall

🖭 LISTENING
Before you listen

Is it usual to rent televisions in your country? What do you do if the television goes wrong? Why is an aerial necessary on a television set?

Listen

A woman goes into a TV rental shop with a complaint. Note the customer's name, address and complaint and the date and time when the engineer can visit.

READING
Before you read

What do you understand by the following expressions?

put up with   out of order   vandalised

Look at the quotations on the right and read what some Americans have to say about the British telephone system. Note down the three complaints they make. Do you agree?

TALKING POINT

In your country, how easy is it to get your telephone repaired, to get a new telephone installed, or to find a public telephone that works?

WRITING
Linking devices: comparison and contrast

Whereas is used to compare and contrast statements of fact.

EXAMPLE

In New York, you can get a telephone fixed within an hour, *whereas* here in Britain it can take days or weeks.

Choose an aspect of everyday life, e.g. education, entertainment, food, transport etc., and compare what you know of the life in Britain, Australia, Canada or the USA with that of your country. Use *whereas* to introduce the comparisons.

'A New Yorker can get a telephone fixed within the hour, even in the evening, whereas here it can take days or weeks to get your phone repaired. Why do the British put up with this service?'

(Ed Malkovich, journalist with Time-Life.)

'In New York, every telephone on every street corner works. In London it's hard to find a public phone that's not out of order or vandalised.'

(Donna Li, a student at the American College.

'We applied three months ago to have a new telephone system installed in our office. We're still waiting.'

(Jo-Ann Pepper, PR consultant.)

Friday Dressing

by Sally Frampton

The idea is simple and attractive. Friday is the day we all begin to relax and look forward to the weekend.

So why not relax the office dress code too and allow workers to wear smart but casual clothes?

It's a philosophy that has been flourishing in America for some time now. It's called 'Friday Dressing'.

But the idea could be potentially dangerous. It's easy enough to dress in the office uniform each day, but when you are free to express yourself one day a week, what do you choose?

The power of clothing cannot be overestimated. Clothes can tell other people a great deal more about us than we realise.

What is daunting about 'Friday Dressing' is that perhaps for the first time your colleagues and superiors can see what you are really like.

The person who looks so cool and superior in a grey or beige fake Armani suit may in fact be a person who likes to relax in lime green tracksuits and purple trainers.

The trouble is that a lack of taste or judgement in clothing is likely to be seen as lack of taste or judgement in business.

Women's clothing is potentially more prob-

Friday feeling: staff at Pareto Partners in conventional business clothes, and, below with a casual look.

lematic than men's. Too tight a dress or too low a neckline will give out the wrong signals. Too much make-up means that you are an exhibitionist; too little means that you can't be bothered. Too loud a colour means you're an attention seeker. Too sober a colour means that you don't dare to take risks.

The trouble with 'Frida Dressing' is that there a no guidelines. One person idea of casual dressing another person's idea sloppy dressing.

For people who lad confidence about the image, 'Friday Dressin may not turn out to be su an attractive idea after all.

-35-

Reading

Before you read

Look at the two photographs.

1 How do the clothes and body language of each person differ between the two photographs?
2 How does this affect your confidence in them as people to do business with?
3 Which sort of clothes would you prefer to work in?

COMPREHENSION

1 Which of the following sentences best sums up the point of the article:

'Friday Dressing'
a) is an American idea which most companies have now adopted with great success.
b) is a good idea because people can express themselves freely through their clothes.
c) is a nice idea in principle but it can be a dangerous one.
d) will never be accepted because there are no guidelines.

2 In what ways can people make mistakes when they wear casual clothes for work?

VOCABULARY

Find the words in the text that mean the same as:

1 rules concerning clothing
2 develop successfully
3 possibly
4 exaggerated
5 discouraging/intimidating
6 imitation
7 a show-off
8 serious, dull
9 careless
10 result in being

THINK ABOUT IT

1 Do you like the idea of 'Friday Dressing'? Does it exist in your country?
2 In pairs or groups, draw up a list of guidelines of *Do's and Don'ts* for a female and male dress code for 'Friday Dressing'.

🖭 LISTENING

Listen to Andrew talking about business people and their image and make notes under the headings:

Traditional image of a businessman	Modern image of a businessman	Modern image of a woman executive

−36−

Grammar

Past modal verbs: *should have*, and *ought to have*

> We're going to be late. We really should have left earlier.

> Well, you shouldn't have talked so long on the phone.

Look at the picture and answer the questions.

1 Why are the couple upset?
2 Why is it the man's fault?

FOCUS

'Should have'/'ought to have'

- These structures are used to criticise actions in the past i.e., to say that something was wrong or done incorrectly:
  We should have/ought to have left earlier. You shouldn't have/oughtn't to have talked so long on the phone.

Points to note
- *Ought to* is more emphatic than *should*.

- These structures also have a continuous form:
  You should have been wearing a seatbelt.

PRACTICE

1 Write sentences for the following situations.

EXAMPLE
1 I've been waiting for hours for you to phone! You should have/ought to have phoned earlier.

2 I told you not to invite Jack. He's always so boring at parties.
3 Look at the time! It's hours past your bedtime.
4 I'm not surprised Mark is ill. All the ice cream is finished.
5 No wonder they're getting divorced. They were only eighteen when they got married.
6 Oh no! I thought she said everyone was going to wear jeans!

2 Say what the people were doing wrong.

EXAMPLE
1 She was driving so fast that she missed the turning off the motorway.
She shouldn't have been driving so fast.

2 He fell off his scooter and hurt his head. Of course, he wasn't wearing his helmet!
3 I suppose you were reading without your glasses? No wonder you've got a headache!
4 Of course the park attendant was angry. You weren't supposed to be walking on the grass!
5 He was cycling without lights. That's why a policeman stopped him.

TALKING POINT

In pairs or groups, discuss who was to blame in this situation and why.

When two seventeen-year-old schoolboys walked into a car showroom in Oxford yesterday and asked to test-drive a new Porsche, a salesman gave them the keys. They drove off at high speed and were later involved in an accident on the motorway. Fortunately nobody was hurt, but the Porsche was a write-off.

WRITING

You came to England to support your football team in an international match. Unfortunately at the match there was a serious outbreak of 'football hooliganism'. Write a letter of complaint to a newspaper, using the notes below to criticise the way the event was organised.
– fans allowed to take drink and bottles into the stadium
– no body search or check for weapons
– alcohol on sale inside the stadium
– fans were not separated

Use this guide:
I am writing to complain about the organisation of . . . on . . . . Firstly, . . . / Secondly . . . /Also . . ./And lastly . . . ./It is not surprising that . . . .

89

37

How far does friendship go?

Ethical choices usually involve love, work, friendship or money – sometimes all four. Occasionally we are faced with a simple decision between good and evil, though usually we find ourselves trying to choose between the lesser of two evils. The distinction between right and wrong is not always clear cut.

David found himself in a personal, professional and ethical dilemma when one of his closest friends learned there was a public relations job coming up in David's company. The friend asked David to recommend him for the job but David didn't think his friend would be able to handle the work.

'I think I could probably help him get the job, but if he weren't my friend I wouldn't recommend him. What if we employed him, at least partly on my say-so, and he was no good? But I really hate to say no to a good friend.'

David made a half-hearted recommendation that revealed his reservations about his friend's capabilities and his friend was satisfied even though he didn't get the job.

But Anne Boe, president of a management consultancy firm, says David handled the situation wrongly. 'I think he should have told his friend the truth – perhaps taken him out to dinner and told him that he wasn't right for the job. I know it's pretty likely that David's friend would be angry with him but there's no easy way out. When you get into a mess of this kind, it's not because you are protecting your friend's feelings but because you're protecting yourself from your friend's anger.'

Glossary
public relations the work of promoting a favourable opinion of an organisation in the mind of the public
say-so (coll) recommendation
management consultancy firm a company which sells advice about management to other organisations

Before you read

Study these words and phrases and say what you think the article on the left will be about.

friend   ask   recommend
job   not able to handle it
dilemma

Words to learn
ethical   handle   half-hearted
reservation   protect

1 Read and answer.

1 How did David's friend want David to help him?
2 Why wasn't David happy about doing this?
3 What ethical choice did David have to make?
4 How did he solve the problem?
5 What should he have done, according to Ann Boe?

2 Read and think.

1 What qualities do you think you need in public relations?
2 How do you think you give a 'half-hearted recommendation'?

3 About you

1 Do you think Anne Boe's criticism was right? Would you tell a friend or close relative the truth if you knew it was going to hurt?
2 Have you ever been asked to lie for a friend? How did it feel? Was it worth it?
3 Do you think 'little white lies' are acceptable?

TALKING POINT

In pairs or groups, discuss what you would do in the following situations.

1 You have just had a meal in a restaurant. The food and the service were very poor. When the bill arrives, you notice the waiter has undercharged you by a pound. Would you point out the mistake or pay the bill and leave?

2 A friend gives you some money and asks you to get him/her some duty-free cigarettes when you are next travelling abroad. You disapprove of smoking. Would you say anything or simply get the cigarettes for your friend?

3 Your sister asks you to say she is ill in bed when her boyfriend phones, but you know that she is going out with another boy that evening. Would you lie for her?

4 You see a job advertised which you would very much like to get. The job demands certain qualifications, one of which you do not have. Would you apply, saying that you had all the qualifications?

VOCABULARY

1 Complete the missing verbs and adjectives in the table below.

NOUN	VERB
decision	decide
qualification	
recommendation	
reservation	

NOUN	ADJECTIVE
ability	able
capability	
possibility	
probability	

2 🔲 Word stress

Words ending in *ion* are stressed on the syllable before the last.

EXAMPLE
decISion

Words ending in *ity* are stressed on the second to last syllable.

EXAMPLE
aBIlity.

Copy the nouns from the Vocabulary exercise and write the stressed syllables in capital letters. Then listen to the tape and repeat the words to see if you were right.

🔲 LISTENING

Before you listen

What does *grant* mean?
What is the difference between an estimate and a bill?

Listen

Dennis, a builder, talks about a recent dilemma. Listen and answer the questions.

1 What did Dennis agree to do?
2 What was the newsagent trying to get from the council?
3 What did the newsagent ask Dennis to do?
4 How did Dennis react?
5 Do you think he did the right thing?

WRITING

Linking devices: contrasting ideas

In formal writing, contrasting ideas can be indicated by *however*.

EXAMPLES
We usually stay at home in the summer. *However,* this year we are going to England.

We usually stay at home in the summer.
This year, *however,* we are going to England.

Notice that *however* can come first in a sentence, or after the word or phrase which it is contrasting.

1 Write pairs of sentences with *however* to express contrast. Use your own ideas.

1 On weekdays . . . at the weekend . . .
2 Now and again . . . most of the time . . .
3 In the past . . . recently . . .
4 I used to think . . .
5 The Mediterranean was once . . .
6 People think that the British . . .
7 Nowadays in Russia . . .
8 In the USA there are . . .

2 Now write some contrasting sentences about where you live, your job and learning English.

38

Communication

Explanation and clarification

🔲 DIALOGUE

Ben is home for the weekend during his last year at college.

MOTHER: What are you doing?
BEN: I'm filling in this application form for a VSO job.
I don't know whether to type it or not.
MOTHER: I would. It looks much better if you type it.
BEN: O.K. Listen, it says here that: 'You may add a supporting statement if you wish.' What does 'a supporting statement' mean?
MOTHER: It's something extra you add to an application form. In other words, you get a chance to say something more about yourself.
BEN: I don't understand why they need more information about me when I've put everything on the form.
MOTHER: Well, it's also an opportunity to say why you think you're suitable for the job. When I worked in the personnel department at ICI it was amazing how many people didn't bother to add one to their CV.
BEN: Well, I suppose I'd better write something then. But I don't know what to say.
MOTHER: You can think of something, surely. You must know why you want the job.
BEN: I'm not sure now. I don't know whether I want it or not.
MOTHER: Ben!

Listen and answer the questions.

1 What is Ben doing?
2 What is his first problem?
3 Why is a supporting statement useful?
4 Why doesn't Ben start to write it?

FOCUS

Explanation/clarification

- Asking for and giving explanations:
  What's a CV?
  It's a curriculum vitae.

  What does 'VSO' stand for?
  It stands for 'Voluntary Service Overseas'.

  What does 'a supporting statement' mean?
  It means something you add to an application form.

- Asking indirectly for advice and help:
  I don't know whether to type it or not.
  I don't know what to say.

- Asking indirectly for clarification:
  I don't understand why they need more information.

PRACTICE

1 In pairs, ask for and give explanations of the following abbreviations.

EXAMPLE
A: What does 'i.e.' mean?
B: It means 'that is' or 'that is to say'.
A: What does 'EFL' stand for?
B: It stands for 'English as a Foreign Language'.

i.e. e.g etc. N.B. P.S. R.S.V.P
EFL UFO EU BBC CIA AIDS

2 In pairs, think of four well-known abbreviations and ask another pair to explain them.

3 Match the expressions below with their correct explanations.

1 out of work
2 a workaholic
3 to work something out
4 hard work
5 shift work
6 social work
7 in working order
8 to have a working knowledge
9 a work permit

a) to have enough practical knowledge to do something
b) work divided into different periods of time
c) work which is difficult or tiring
d) official permission to work in a country
e) unemployed
f) a person who is unable to stop working
g) to find the answer to a problem
h) functioning without any problems
i) work done to help people in poor social conditions

4 Now practise asking for and giving explanations for the expressions in Exercise 3, using the following:

What's . . .? What does . . . mean? Could you tell me/Could you explain what . . . means? It means . . ./I'm afraid I don't know what it means.

5 You are applying for a credit card. You don't understand why certain information is required by the finance company. Use the headings on the form to question the information.

EXAMPLE
I don't understand why they need to know how many children I've got./if I've got any children.

Address	
Telephone numbers Home	/
Business	/
Married ☐ **Single** ☐ **Widowed** ☐ **Divorced** ☐	
No. of children aged 11-18 ☐ **3-10** ☐ **Under 3** ☐	
Your occupation	
Gross income	**Monthly income**
	Tenant

6 Look at the advertisement above. You are interested in the job as Play Leader but you are not sure how to write the letter or what to put in it. Discuss the queries with your partner.

EXAMPLE
A: I don't know how to write the date in English.
B: You write it like this – 16th February.
A: I don't know whether to . . .

1 How do I write the date in English?
2 Do I write my name at the top of the letter or not?
3 Where do I put the name and address of the person I'm writing to?
4 How do I start the letter?
5 How do I end the letter?
6 Do I include a CV or not?

WRITING

Write a letter applying for the job as Play Leader. Say why you think you are suitable for the job. Give details of any relevant experience you have had with children and say when you would be available for interview.

🔲 LISTENING

1 Listen to a man enrolling on an English course and note what he says when he asks for information or clarification.
2 Listen again. When you hear 'bleep', ask for the same information, using the language taken from this lesson.

39

Grammar

Past modal verbs:
could have, might have, must have and can't have

Answer the questions.

1 Do Laura's friends know why she is late?
2 What does one of the men think has happened?
3 What does the woman think has happened? Why?
4 Why does the man disagree?

FOCUS
'May/might/could/must/can't have'

I He She It We You They	may might could can't must	have	seen it. bought it. done it. finished it.

- *May/might/could have* are used when the speaker is speculating about the past:
  She could have had a late meeting at the office.
  She may/might have got the wrong day.
  These are all similar in meaning.

- *Must have/can't have* are used when the speaker is drawing a conclusion about something that happened in the past:
  She must have forgotten about this evening.
  She can't have forgotten.

Note
These structures also have a continuous form.
She might/must/can't have been waiting all morning.

What's the difference in meaning?

1 He might have left his glasses on the table.
2 He must have left his glasses on the table.
3 He can't have left his glasses on the table.

PRACTICE

1 Complete the sentences using *must have* or *can't have* and the verb in brackets.

EXAMPLE

1 She didn't answer the door bell even though I rang several times.
She . . . (be) asleep.
She must have been asleep.

2 I . . . (run out of) petrol. I only filled up the tank this morning.

3 I'm so sorry I'm late. You . . . (wonder) what had happened.

4 Cathy's got a new BMW! She . . . (win) a lottery.

5 I . . . (lose) my glasses. They were here a minute ago.

6 The flowers are beautiful! They . . . (cost) you a fortune.

7 Alan . . . (get lost). I gave him the address and drew a map.

2 Gerry is late for a business meeting. Speculate about what has happened to him using the notes below.

get caught in a traffic jam – watch/stop – car/break down – forget the day – oversleep – have accident

EXAMPLE
He may/might/could have got caught in a traffic jam.

ACT IT OUT

Telephone to find out if Gerry has left home.

GERRY	YOU
Answer the phone.	
	Ask Gerry why he isn't at the meeting.
Apologise and explain that you aren't feeling well.	
	Say what you thought might have happened.
Explain that you were sick all night and that it must have been something you ate.	
	Tell Gerry what you think he should have done.
Apologise and say when you'll be able to get in to work.	

AA ★★★

The Salisbury Hotel

RAC ★★★

Mrs Sheila Nesbitt
Assistant Manager

Salisbury, Wiltshire tel: 0722 3891

Children and dogs welcome.

WRITING

You think you must have left your diary at The Salisbury Hotel when you stayed there recently. You are not sure if you left it in your room or in reception when you were making a phone call. Write a letter to the hotel manager and explain. Lay out your letter formally and include the necessary addresses and today's date. Start your letter *Dear Mrs Nesbitt* and end *Yours sincerely* and your name.

PARAGRAPH 1
Say when you were a guest at the hotel and why you are writing.
PARAGRAPH 2
Describe the diary and any identifying features it has. Give any helpful suggestions as to where and how you might have lost it.
PARAGRAPH 3
Ask the manager to forward the diary if she finds it.

🖭 LISTENING

mug² *v* -gg- [T] to rob (a person) with violence, esp. in a public place —**mugging** *n* [C;U]: *a big increase in the number of muggings in this area*

Before you listen

1 Have you ever been mugged or do you know anyone who has?
2 What effect has the incident had on you or the person you know?
3 Find out the meaning of the following words:
attack   vulnerable   assault
bump into   ashamed

Listen

You are going to hear about a mugging incident on Charing Cross Bridge, in London. Make notes under these headings:
Who? When? Where? What? How? What effect?

About the author

Maya Angelou started writing quite late in life. She was forty-one when her first novel: *I Know Why the Caged Bird Sings* was published. She was born in 1928 in St Louis, Missouri. After the break-up of her parents' marriage, she and her brother went to live with their grandmother but later moved to California to live with their mother. At sixteen, Maya gave birth to her son, Guy. In the years that followed, she was a waitress, singer, actress, dancer and black activist as well as a mother. The scene that follows is taken from her second book: *Gather Together in My Name*.

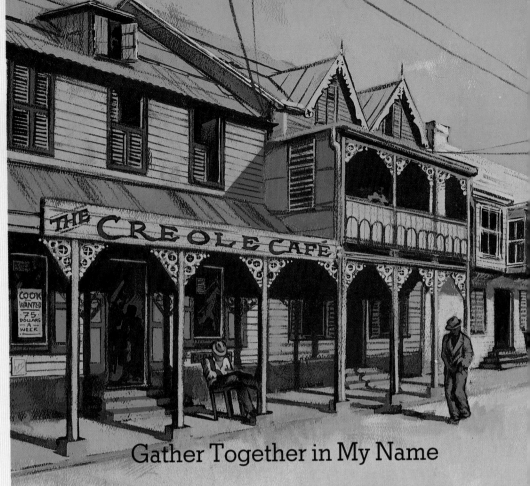

Gather Together in My Name

'Can you cook Creole?'

I looked at the woman and gave her a lie as soft as melting butter.

'Yes, of course. That's all I know how to cook.'

The Creole Café had a cardboard sign in the window which said: *Cook wanted. Seventy-five dollars a week*. As soon as I saw it I knew I could cook Creole, whatever that was.

Desperation to find help must have blinded the woman to my age or perhaps it was the fact that I was nearly six feet and had an attitude which belied my seventeen years. She didn't question me about recipes and menus, but doubt hung on the edge of her questions.

'Can you start on Monday?'

'I'll be glad to.'

'You know it's six days a week. We're closed on Sunday.'

'That's fine with me. I like to go to church on Sunday.'

It's awful to think that the devil gave me that lie, but it came unexpectedly and worked like dollar bills. Suspicion and doubt raced from her face, and she smiled.

'Well, I know we're going to get along. You're a good Christian. I like that. Yes, ma'am, I sure do.'

My need for a job caught and held the denial.

'What time on Monday?'

'You get here at five.'

Five in the morning!

'All right, I'll be here at five, Monday morning.'

Mrs Dupree was a short plump woman of about fifty. Her hair was naturally straight and heavy.

'And what's your name?'

'Rita.' Marguerite was too solemn, and Maya too rich-sounding. 'Rita' sounded like dark flashing eyes, hot peppers and Creole evenings with strummed guitars. 'Rita Johnson.'

'That's a right nice name.' Then, like some people do to show their sense of familiarity, she immediately narrowed the name down.

'I'll call you Reet. Okay?'

Okay, of course. I had a job. Seventy-five dollars a week. So I was Reet. All Reet. Now all I had to do was learn to cook.

Glossary

black activist someone actively fighting for the rights and freedoms of black people

Creole hot, spicy food of French origin typical of the southern USA

belied gave a false idea of

Reading

Guess the meaning

doubt   suspicion   get along   denial
solemn   familiarity

COMPREHENSION

1 Answer the questions.

1 What sort of food did the café specialise in?
2 How much money would Maya get?
3 How many days a week would she work?
4 Did she get the job?
5 What time did she have to get to the café in the morning?
6 Why did she like the name Rita? What was her real name in full?
7 What did Mrs Dupree want to call her?
8 How many lies did Maya tell?

2 Complete the sentences correctly.

1 Maya:
a) knew how to cook Creole food.
b) pretended she knew how to cook Creole food.
c) never cooked anything but Creole food.

2 The woman in the café:
a) knew Maya was seventeen.
b) thought she might be seventeen.
c) thought she was older than seventeen.

3 The woman asked Maya:
a) if she could start on Monday.
b) what recipes she knew.
c) if she was a Christian.

4 Maya:
a) went to church every Sunday.
b) went to church on another day of the week.
c) wasn't a regular churchgoer.

5 The woman was more sure about Maya when Maya told her that she:
a) went to church.
b) didn't mind getting up at five.
c) could cook Creole food.

6 The woman shortened the name Rita to Reet because:
a) she thought Rita sounded too solemn.
b) she thought it was too long.
c) she wanted to sound friendly.

THINK ABOUT IT

1 Would you describe Maya's story as sad, amusing or silly?
2 Do you think Maya's lies were serious?

STYLE
Imaginative description

One way in which writers make their descriptions vivid and exciting is by using similes and metaphors. Remember that a simile compares one thing to another by using *like* or *as*, e.g. *She acted like a maniac. His hands were as cold as ice.*

A metaphor also compares things but doesn't use *like* or *as*. It describes something with words that are usually used to describe something else, e.g. *The sun reached out and stroked my face.*

Reread the text. How does how Maya Angelou express the following ideas?

1 I told a lie smoothly.
2 Her questions contained doubt.
3 Suddenly there was no sign of doubt or suspicion on her face.
4 I so badly needed a job that I didn't deny that I was a Christian.
5 Rita was an exciting-sounding name.

TALKING POINT

What problems do you think Maya Angelou might have had as a black, unmarried mother living in San Francisco in the early 1940s?

WRITING

Look at the text about the author, Maya Angelou, then use the following notes to write a short biography about Carson McCullers, a white woman who wrote about the 'Deep South' of the USA.

```
Carson McCullers

American writer (1917-67)

- first book/aged 23/'The Heart
  is a Lonely Hunter' (1940)

- born Columbus, Georgia/
  originally wanted to be a musician

- married at 20/difficult marriage/ended
  in husband's suicide 1953

- established reputation as a writer with
  'Reflections in a Golden Eye' (1941),
  and 'Member of the Wedding' (1946)

- in spite of ill-health and alcoholism,
  wrote until her death in 1967
```

Check

1 Match the two halves of the sentences.

1 If I were you,
2 If they knew where she was,
3 I wouldn't take the job,
4 Would you go to China,
5 If you left at five,
6 What would you do with the money,

a) if they offered you a job there?
b) you'd get there by six.
c) they wouldn't worry so much.
d) if you won?
e) I'd get a new one.
f) if I were you.

2 Write the correct form of the verbs in brackets.

1 If you (not know) he was English, you would never guess.
2 If you found £10 in the street, (you/give) it to the police?
3 I (not/wear) jeans if I were you.
4 You (get) there on time if you took the five o'clock train.

5 If I (have) a rest now, I'd fall asleep.
6 A: (you/marry) him if he asked you?
   B: No, I (not/marry) him if he (be) the last man on earth!
7 If they (not want) to come, they'd say so.
8 She (not mind) if you used the phone.

3 Complete the second half of the sentences.

1 You'll break it if (you/be/not) careful.
2 I wouldn't go unless (I/have to).
3 If you drink that water (you/be) ill.

4 Would you feel better if (she/apologise)?
5 The cat won't eat the fish unless (you/cook) it.
6 What would you say if (I/phone) the police?

4 Rewrite the questions starting with the phrases provided.

1 Where's John?
  Have you any idea . . .
2 How do I get to the station from here?
  Could you tell me . . .
3 When does the next programme start?
  Can you tell me . . .
4 Have we got any homework?
  Do you know . . .

5 What time does the last underground train leave?
  Have you any idea . . .
6 Did Sam paint that picture?
  Do you know . . .
7 Why is everyone laughing?
  Could you tell me . . .
8 Where is the nearest public phone box?
  Can you tell me . . .

5 Choose the right verb below to write short sentences using *I'd like* and the cues provided.

take away   clean   repair   service   type   cut   paint   install   check   wash

EXAMPLE
1 I'd like my car serviced, please.

1 my car   3 my hair   5 this leather jacket   7 my windscreen   9 the door
2 this watch   4 these letters   6 all that rubbish   8 this computer system   10 the tyres

6 Choose the best answer.

1 I'd like to book an appointment to:
a) have my hair cut.
b) cut my hair.
c) have cut my hair.

2 I'll:
a) have someone to fix it immediately.
b) get fixed immediately.
c) have it fixed immediately.

3 I'd like this £5 note:
a) to have it changed, please.
b) changing, please.
c) changed, please.

7 Choose the correct verb form in these sentences.

1 You *should see/should have seen* his face when I told him!
2 When you visit Florence, *you ought to go/ought to have gone* to see the Uffizi gallery.
3 You *shouldn't have taken/shouldn't take* my camera on holiday with you. I was very angry.
4 It's a pity we didn't ask Kelly. We *should think/should have thought* of it earlier.
5 You *ought to write/ought to have written* a book about it soon.

8 Rewrite the following sentences using *should have* or *shouldn't have* and the past participle of the verb.

1 It was wrong of you to keep the change. (You . . .)
2 I'm sorry I got so angry. (I . . .)
3 How stupid of them not to check the time of the train. (They . . .)
4 Why didn't I take my swimming things? (I . . .)
5 The accident was his fault. He was drinking and driving. (He . . .)

9 Complete the sentences using *might have, must have* or *can't have,* and the correct form of the verb in brackets.

1 I can't find my keys anywhere. I think I . . . (lose) them.
2 You shouldn't have driven when it was so foggy. You . . . (have) an accident.
3 You never know. They . . . (take) the wrong bus.
4 She . . . (telephone) because I was in all day.
5 I'm glad you didn't come to see me yesterday. You . . . (catch) my cold.
6 I . . . (lose) my passport. It was here on the table just a few minutes ago.

10 Choose the best answer.

1 TEACHER: Today we are going to read about Mary, who's a physiotherapist.
   STUDENT: Excuse me, but
   a) what means 'physiotherapist'?
   b) can you tell me what 'physiotherapist' means, please?
   c) could you tell me what does 'physiotherapist' mean?

2 TEACHER: What's the matter, Louis? Why aren't you writing anything?
   STUDENT: I don't know
   a) what should I write?
   b) what I am writing.
   c) what to write.

3 STUDENT: But I don't understand
   a) why you can't use the present tense.
   b) why can't you use the present tense.
   c) why it's not possible the present tense.

11 Match the phrasal verb in column A with its more formal equivalent in column B.

A
1 put up with
2 put in
3 put out (of fire)
4 take back
5 go away
6 set up

B
a return
b extinguish
c suffer
d start
e install
f leave

12 What would you say in the following situations?

1 You are at a railway station and want to know which platform the train for Bristol leaves from. You ask a porter.

2 You have torn your best suede jacket. You have seen a notice at the dry cleaner's saying: 'We do alterations and repairs' so you take your jacket along.

3 A travel agent advises you to buy an Apex ticket. You have never heard of this type of ticket before and ask for an explanation.

4 A teacher is leaving at the end of term and you have been asked to give a short speech at her leaving party. You go to a friend for help.

5 You have offered to walk home with a friend after a party but your friend wants to walk home alone. You are puzzled.

Use your English

1 Look at the scene at the airport and in pairs, complete the polite requests in the bubbles. Don't worry – there are several different ways of completing each request.

EXAMPLE

1 Can you tell me what the exchange rate is for the dollar?

2 (Student B: page 128)
In Part 1 you have a list of half completed conditional sentences. In Part 2 you have a list of possible endings for Student B's sentences. You read your first sentence and Student B must choose a suitable ending from his/her list using the correct form of the verb. Then Student B reads one of his/her sentences for you to complete.

EXAMPLE

A: If I got £100 for my birthday,…

B: I'd spend it on a pair of roller blades.

B: If I could go anywhere in the world …

Part 1 (uncompleted sentences)

If I got £100 for my birthday, I …
If I saw someone stealing in a shop, I …
If I suddenly lost my job, I …
I would be very surprised if I …
I would dive into ice cold water if you …
Would you live abroad if you …

Part 2 (possible endings for Student B's sentences)

see what's happened to his car.
come with me?
go to Bali.
know something about computers.
save my photograph album.
be rich and good-looking?

3 (Student B: page 128)
Complete the information in your chart by asking Student B which jobs Stuart likes to do himself and which he likes to have done by someone else. Then it's Student B's turn to ask you about Ruth.

EXAMPLE

A: What does Stuart do about servicing his car?

B: He usually has it serviced.

JOBS	Ruth		Stuart	
	HERSELF	SOMEONE ELSE	HIMSELF	SOMEONE ELSE
service the car	✓			
alter his/her clothes		✓		
type his/her letters		✓		
cut his/her hair		✓		
decorate the house		✓		
clean the house	✓			

4 In pairs, read the account of a disastrous day and find explanations for each situation marked * using a sentence with *can't have* or *must have*.**

EXAMPLE

1 You can't have got the correct timetable.
 or You must have got an out-of-date timetable.

Your timetable says that there is a train leaving for your destination at 11 a.m. but you have to wait half an hour before it comes. (1) ***

You telephone your friends to say that you will be late. Their answerphone is switched on. (2) ***

You leave a message. When you finally get on the train, you notice that the carriage you are sitting in is very dirty with sweet papers and orange juice cans everywhere. (3) ***

When you arrive at your destination, you realise that your friends are not there at the station to meet you as arranged. (4) ***

You take a taxi to their house and your friends are delighted to see you. Apparently their car had broken down so they couldn't meet you.

But your troubles haven't ended. When you unpack you can't find your hairbrush and comb. (5) ***

You also notice that your bottle of shampoo has leaked all over your clothes. (6) ***

You are not sure if you want the weekend to continue!

Progress test

Units 31–40

GRAMMAR

1 Choose the correct answer.

Seventeen-year-old Jason is getting ready to go out with his girlfriend, Lisa. His mother is in his room.

MOTHER: I ...(1)... wear those trousers if I were you.
a) don't   b) won't   c) wouldn't

JASON: Why not?

MOTHER: They look a bit short to me.

JASON: Well, they were all right last week. You ...(2)... them in the wash.
a) must shrink   b) must have shrunk
c) must have been shrunk

MOTHER: You ...(3)... put them in the wash at all. They need drycleaning.
a) shouldn't have   b) oughtn't to
c) shouldn't

JASON: Well, I'll have to wear jeans then. By the way, have you any idea where ...(4)...?
a) is my red shirt   b) my red shirt is
c) my red shirt

MOTHER: Have you looked in the wardrobe?

JASON: I've looked everywhere. In my wardrobe. In the wash. In my cupboard.

MOTHER: Well, you ...(5)... lost it. It was here yesterday.
a) can't have   b) mustn't have
c) shouldn't have

Wait a minute. What's this under the bed?

JASON: Oh, thanks. Oh no, it needs ironing.

MOTHER: I can't understand why ...(6)... everything until the last minute.
a) do you leave   b) are you leaving
c) you leave

Give it to me.

JASON: No, it's O.K. I'll do it.

MOTHER: And I think your hair's getting a bit long too. When are you going to ...(7)...?
a) have cut it   b) have it cut
c) having it cut

JASON: Mum! Stop nagging! Anyway, I haven't got ...(8)... to go to the hairdresser's.
a) much money   b) enough money
c) money enough

Now, if you ...(9)... me £10, I'd go tomorrow.
a) lend   b) would lend   c) lent

MOTHER: Come on. Lisa will be here in a minute. Give that shirt to me.

JASON: What ...(10)... I do without you, Mum?
a) do   b) would   c) can

MOTHER: I don't know. I really don't know.

VOCABULARY

2 Find the odd word out.

1 ring   bracelet   shirt   necklace
2 violent   harmless   aggressive   unscrupulous
3 brakes   tyres   windscreen   petrol
4 spend   wash   invest   save
5 road   scooter   motorbike   car
6 builder   carpenter   tailor   decorator
7 fix   destroy   mend   repair
8 vandalised   destroyed   mugged   ruined

3 What are the opposites of these words? Choose from these prefixes: *un-, in-, im-, dis-*.

dependent
forgettable
personal
able
honest
happy
scrupulous
possible
acceptable

USAGE

4 Complete each of the numbered gaps in the text from the list below.

for   hobby   but   eventually   worse   hated
agreement   up   might   down   computer   to
broke   example   promise   amount

Young people who are fed ...(1)... with their parents nagging about the state of their room should try and work out the minimum ...(2)... of change that will satisfy them both. The story of Doug is a good ...(3)... .

Doug hated his mother coming into his room ...(4)... realised that it was absolutely necessary to vacuum clean his room. His ...(5)... was computers and he knew that dust ...(6)... interfere with his equipment. He and his mother ...(7)... worked out a compromise. They came to an ...(8)... about what she was responsible ...(9)... in his room and what he was responsible for. They wrote it all ...(10)... and signed it. They decided that if Doug ...(11)... the agreement he would be 'sentenced' ...(12)... read one of his mother's women's magazines, which he ...(13)... . If she failed to keep her ...(14)..., she would have to read one of his ...(15)... magazines, which she could not understand. Neither could think of a ...(16)... penalty for the other.

Errol

A police officer

SO YOU WANT TO JOIN THE POLICE?

Fay Rowan interviews Errol Mason, a young police officer from Bristol.

WHEN I CONTACTED Police Constable Errol Mason, he was just finishing a nine-day night shift and was understandably trying to catch up on lost sleep. 'It's hard to sleep during the day but you just have to try,' said Errol, 'otherwise you end up exhausted.'

I asked him when we could meet for a chat. 'What about coming along to the ice rink on Tuesday evening – say, about eight?' he suggested. Errol told me that he spent most of his free time playing ice hockey. So the following Tuesday evening I sat and watched Errol skating across the ice. Later, over a cup of coffee, I asked him what his job in the police involved.

'Many people have only one image of the police. They think we spend our time chasing criminals in fast cars with wailing sirens and flashing lights,' said Errol with a grin. 'In fact, that's only one small part of the job. A lot of police work can be quite boring. You can be on the desk doing routine office work for a whole month at a time. Then the next month you may be driving around on patrol. Then, perhaps you're "on the beat" for a bit.'

Errol told me that one of the most interesting parts of the job was in fact 'community policing'. I asked him what this involved. 'You have your own special area which you have to patrol. It really means being on the beat: walking round keeping your eyes open, making sure you know what's going on, chatting to people, basically trying to prevent crime.'

Thinking of some of the recent ugly scenes at football matches and demonstrations, I asked Errol if he was conscious of the dangers involved and if he was ever frightened. 'Sometimes, yes,' he replied. 'Anyone would be. It's just one of the things you learn to accept. Violence is always frightening and a lot more people nowadays are carrying weapons — knives, coshes and so on. Except in extreme circumstances, all we carry are truncheons, handcuffs and a radio.' When I asked if the irregular hours of police work affected his social life, Errol smiled. 'My girlfriend gets a bit annoyed – she says I'm either on night shift or I'm playing ice hockey! But it's not like being a doctor. When you're off duty, that's it. It has to be a real emergency like a major riot or something to be called out on your night off.'

If you think police work sounds like the job for you, write for more information.

Glossary
cosh a short solid rubber or metal tube used as a weapon
truncheon a short stick carried as a weapon by the police
handcuffs a pair of metal rings joined by a short chain for holding together the wrists of a prisoner

Words to learn

exhausted   chase   criminal (n)   grin (n)
patrol (n)   demonstration   off duty
emergency   riot

1 Read and find out:

1 where and when the interviewer met Errol
2 what people think the police spend most of
   their time doing.
3 what equipment Errol carries.

2 Choose the right answer.

1 According to Errol the best part of his job is:
a) working on night shift.
b) driving around in fast cars.
c) doing 'community policing.'

2 He thinks his job is:
a) more ordinary than people imagine.
b) more exciting than people imagine.
c) easier than people imagine.

3 He says that police work is more dangerous
   nowadays because:
a) there are so many more football matches
   and demonstrations.
b) more people are carrying dangerous
   weapons.
c) the police only carry a truncheon and
   handcuffs.

4 Errol's girlfriend is annoyed because:
a) he doesn't spend enough time with her.
b) he's always being called out when
   he's off duty.
c) he never gets any time off.

3 Read and think.

1 Why is working a nightshift more tiring than
   working a dayshift?
2 How do you think people get their image of
   the police?
3 Why do you think Errol finds going on the
   beat interesting?
4 Why do you think the police carry radios?
5 What do you think is an example of 'an
   extreme circumstance'?

4 About you

1 Have you ever had to report an incident to
   the police?
2 Do you know any police officers personally?
   What are they like when they're off duty?

VOCABULARY

**1 In what ways are the following crimes
similar? What do they each involve?**

burglary   shoplifting   robbery
pickpocketing   mugging

2 Copy and complete the list.

PERSON	CRIME	PERSON	CRIME
burglar	burglary	. . .	shoplifting
. . .	crime	. . .	smuggling
. . .	theft	. . .	murder
. . .	robbery	. . .	pickpocketing
. . .	rape	. . .	drug dealing

**3 ▣ Listen to the following compound
nouns. Copy them, writing the stressed
syllables in capital letters.**

police officer   police station
drug smuggling   armed robbery
community policing   criminal investigation

EXAMPLE
poLICE   OFFicer

TALKING POINT

1 What aspects of police work do you think are
   dangerous or unpleasant?
2 Do you think the police treat all sections of
   society in the same way?
3 What is the public image of the police in your
   country? Is it accurate?

▣ LISTENING

Listen to a police officer talking about her work.
How does she describe the shift system? What
does she think is the most unpleasant part of
her job? Why?

−42−

Grammar

Reported speech (1)

Look at the sentences.

1 'I spend most of my free time playing ice hockey,' he said.
2 He said that he spent most of his free time playing ice hockey.

Which sentence is in direct speech and which is in reported speech? What happens to the tense of the verb *spend* in reported speech? What other differences are there between the two sentences? Find examples of reported speech in the text about Errol. Which are reported statements and which are reported questions? Check with the Focus section below.

Reported statements

DIRECT STATEMENT	REPORTED STATEMENT
'I'm a police officer.'	*He said/told me (that) he was a police officer.*
'I live in Bristol.'	*He said/told me (that) he lived in Bristol.*

Reported questions

DIRECT QUESTION	REPORTED QUESTION
'When can we meet?'	*I asked (him) when we could meet.*
'Are you ever frightened?'	*She asked if he was ever frightened.*

> ### FOCUS
>
> - Reported speech is often introduced by *say* and *tell*.
>
> - *Tell* is always followed by a name or an object pronoun:
>   *He told me he was a police officer.*
>
> - When the reporting verb is in the present tense, there is no change in the tense:
>   *'I don't want to come.'*
>   *He says he doesn't want to come.*
>
> - *That* is always optional after verbs of speaking.
>
> - In reported questions the word order of the original question is changed:
>   *'What's your name?'*
>   *She asked what my name was.*

Verb changes

am/is – was

are – were

am/is going to – was going to

have/has – had

go – went

went – had gone

have gone – had gone

can – could

will – would

shall – should

may – might

must – had to

The tense of the verb in the direct speech usually 'moves' further back into the past.

Other changes

today	that day
tonight	that night
tomorrow	the next day
yesterday	the day before
ago	before
last week	the week before
next week	the following week
this/that	the
this morning	that morning
here	there

I spend most of my free time playing ice hockey.

PRACTICE

1 Rewrite the following statements in reported speech.

EXAMPLE

1 'I'm going to watch television,' he said to his mother.
   He told his mother (that) he was going to watch television.

2 'We moved to Bristol three years ago,' said the woman.
   She said . . .

3 'I'll come at eight tomorrow,' she said.
   She told me . . .

4 'I've bought a new car,' she said.
   She said . . .

5 'I can't think of anything to write,' said the boy to his teacher.
   The boy told . . .

6 'We're driving the car to France next summer,' they said.
   They said . . .

7 'I must get some new glasses,' he said.
   He said that . . .

8 'I may sell my bicycle,' she said.
   She said . . .

2 Answer these questions about Errol using reported speech in the past. What did Errol say about:

1 sleeping after a night-shift?
2 community policing?
3 the equipment he carries?

3 Errol is on duty at the police station. Read or listen to the dialogue and find out what the man has lost, where and when.

▣ DIALOGUE

MAN: I've lost my briefcase. Has one been handed in this morning?

ERROL: No, sir, it hasn't. Where did you lose it?

MAN: Outside my house in Chester Street this morning. I put it on the pavement, then I drove away and forgot about it.

ERROL: Can you describe the briefcase, sir?

MAN: Yes, it's black leather with a combination lock and it has my initials D.B. on it.

ERROL: Is there anything valuable inside it?

MAN: No, there isn't. Just a few papers and some computer discs.

ERROL: Well, we'll let you know if we hear anything about it. Can I have your name and phone number please?

4 Work in pairs. In turn, report the conversation between the man and Errol using reported questions and statements.

A: A man came in and said he had lost . . . He asked if . . .

B: Errol asked him where . . .

WRITING

Complete Errol's report about the missing briefcase.

LOST PROPERTY REPORT
Time: 10 a.m. Date: Monday, 13th June . . .
Item missing: one briefcase with personal contents

At approximately 10 a.m. this morning Mr D. Barton reported the loss of a briefcase . . . . .
Mr Barton said he . . . . .

BRISTOL POLICE
Lost & Found Property Book

-43-

Communication

Closing strategies

💾 **DIALOGUE 1** Outside college

MIKE: Are you going to Steve's party tonight?
NICKY: No, I'm not that keen on parties. Look, I really ought to be going now. I've got some work to do. I've got an essay to write before tomorrow.
MIKE: O.K. Look, I'll give you a ring about lunch sometime.
NICKY: Yes, O.K. Listen, I really have to go now.
MIKE: I know. Good luck with your essay.
NICKY: Thanks. I'll need it. Bye now. Have a good time at the party.
MIKE: Thanks. Bye. Take care.

💾 **DIALOGUE 2** In a café

TESSA: I was really angry with him.
SALLY: I don't blame you.
TESSA: Oh no! Look at the time. I've got to go. It's getting late. My parents want me home by six.
SALLY: I suppose I'd better go too.
TESSA: Listen, why don't we meet later on this evening?
SALLY: O.K. Let's do that. Give me a ring at home at about nine.
TESSA: Right. Bye for now. See you later.

Read or listen to the dialogues and find out:

1 how the different people signal that they want to end the conversation and what reasons they give.
2 how the other person responds in each case.
3 what arrangements they make for further contact.
4 what leave-taking phrases are used.

FOCUS

Closing strategies

- Ending conversations:
  Look, I really ought to be going now.
  Listen, I really have to go now.
  Look at the time. I've got to go.

- Giving a reason:
  I've got some work to do.
  It's getting late.

- Making arrangements to make contact again:
  I'll give you a ring about lunch some time.
  Why don't we meet later on this evening?

- Leave-taking phrases:
  See you (later/soon/on Monday)
  Good luck with/on …
  Give my regards to …
  Have a good time/evening/ weekend!
  Take care.
  Bye (for now)!

PRACTICE

1 Match the leave-taking phrases with an appropriate response.

1 See you soon.
2 Good luck with the exam.
3 Look, I really must be going.
4 Give my regards to Ann.
5 Have a good holiday!
6 Bye for now.
7 Take care.

a) Yes, and give mine to Pat.
b) I will. Don't worry.
c) Thanks. I'll need it.
d) Yes, see you.
e) Yes, bye.
f) Yes, I must go too.
g) Thanks and the same to you.

2 In pairs, practise ending conversations.

Signal that you want to end the conversation. Give a reason. Make arrangements to make contact some other time, and take your leave.

REASONS FOR ENDING A CONVERSATION:

It's getting late.
You think there's someone at the door.
Someone's coming to see you in a minute.
You've got some work to do.
You've got to telephone someone else.
Someone else wants to use the phone.

EXAMPLE

A: Listen, I really have to go. It's getting late.
B: Yes, I suppose I'd better go too.
A: Look, why don't I call you tomorrow?
B: O.K. Well, have a nice evening.
A: Thanks and the same to you.

🔲 LISTENING

Listen to four conversations and match them to the correct pictures below.

WRITING
Ending informal letters

Well, I must stop now and catch the post.
Well, I think that's all the news.
I'll stop now as it's getting late.

Closing phrases

Look after yourself.
Give my love/regards to . . .
With best wishes, . . .
Write soon.
All my love, . . ./Love, . . .

Use the following guide to write a letter to a friend.

PARAGRAPH 1
Thank your friend for a recent letter and apologise for not writing earlier. Explain why you have been busy.

PARAGRAPH 2
Tell your friend if you are enjoying your English classes or not, and say which lessons you have enjoyed most. Report any special news.

PARAGRAPH 3
Ask your friend for news about home, holidays and family.

PARAGRAPH 4
Give a reason for ending your letter and send regards to any people who know you. Ask your friend to write back as soon as possible.

'Sorry this is so short but I must catch the post!'

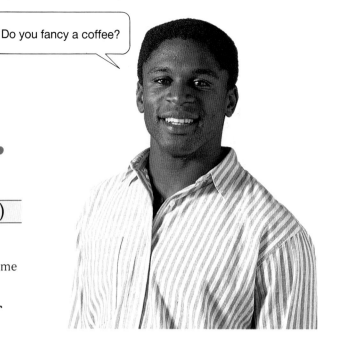

Do you fancy a coffee?

—44—

Grammar

Reported speech (2)

When I met Errol at the ice rink, he offered me a coffee.

How many different ways can you offer someone a cup of coffee in English?

FOCUS

Verbs of reporting

Apart from *say, tell* and *ask,* there are many other verbs which report speech.
Here are some of them with the structures which follow them:

- **Verb + object + infinitive**
  advise   remind
  ask   tell
  persuade   warn
  He advised me to leave at once.
  He warned me not to stay.

- **Verb + two objects**
  introduce   offer
  She introduced her husband to me.
  He offered me a coffee.

- **Verb + infinitive**
  agree refuse promise
  They agreed to come.

- **Verb + that + clause**
  say explain
  I explained that I wasn't feeling well.

- **Verb + *ing* form**
  suggest
  He suggested meeting at the rink.

- **Verb + preposition + *ing* form**
  apologise
  He apologised for being rude.

- **Verb + object**
  accept refuse
  I accepted the invitation.

PRACTICE

1 Match the reported speech with the actual words spoken.

REPORTED SPEECH

1 She advised him to get a summer job.
2 She warned him not to drive too fast.
3 He reminded her not to drive too fast.
4 She persuaded her to come.
5 He told them not to be late.
6 She suggested going for a coffee.
7 I offered to help them.
8 He refused to help them.
9 I invited her to lunch.
10 She apologised for being late.
11 She agreed to ask him.
12 He introduced Mary to his colleague.

WORDS SPOKEN

a) 'Mary, meet my friend, Gill.'
b) 'Would you like me to help you?'
c) 'I'm sorry I'm late.'
d) 'If I were you, I'd get a summer job.'
e) 'O.K., I'll ask him.'
f) 'Don't drive too fast. This road is dangerous.'
g) A: Oh, please come! B: Oh, all right then.
h) 'Don't be late!'
i) 'Why don't we go for a coffee?'
j) 'I'm not going to help you.'
k) 'Would you like to come to lunch?'
l) 'Don't forget there's a speed limit here.'

2 Read the following dialogues and choose the verb which best describes the actual words spoken.

1 MIKE: Would you like to come with Greg and me to the open-air concert on Saturday?
a) apologise b) offer c) invite

JANE: Brilliant! I'd love to come.
a) accept b) refuse c) remind

2 BEN: What should I do about my briefcase?
a) agree b) ask c) introduce

SUE: Why don't you go to the police station and report it?
a) offer b) tell c) suggest

3 MARK: Mum, please can we go to the carnival? We'll be all right! You know we will!
a) try to persuade b) try to agree c) warn

MUM: O.K., but don't take a lot of money in case there are pickpockets around.
a) agree but remind b) agree but warn c) refuse

3 Report the conversations using the correct verb of reported speech.

EXAMPLE
Mike invited Jane to a concert, and she . . .

▣ LISTENING

Before you listen

If people who have young children want to go out, what arrangements can they make?

Listen

1 Two people are talking about a broken arrangement.

Note:
what Alan was going to do.
where Paul and his wife were going.
what time Alan arrived.
what excuse Alan made.
how Paul felt when Alan finally arrived.

2 Listen again and note the verbs of reporting in the order in which they occur.

WRITING

Write a paragraph from Paul's letter to a friend reporting how Alan let him down the other evening. Use the verbs of reporting that you listed in the Listening exercise.

Start like this:
I'm writing this in a very bad mood. You remember Alan? Well, he really let us down the other evening. We had tickets for . . .

ACT IT OUT

In pairs, use the information above to act out a conversation about a visit to a nightclub.

A
You want to go to a fashionable new nightclub which has opened in a run-down part of the city. You want B to go with you to try it out. Explain that the area isn't really dangerous but suggest going to the club by taxi. Try to persuade your friend to go with you as you do not want to go alone.

B
You have heard about the new nightclub but are not keen to go there because a friend of yours was mugged in that part of the city a few weeks ago and you don't want to go anywhere near it. Besides, you have to start work early in the morning. Agree or refuse to go as you wish.

Reading

The changing role of the police

COMPREHENSION

1 Match the headlines with the correct newspaper article.

1 POLICE HALT NURSES' MARCH
2 POLICE WARNING TO ARMED GANGS
3 POLICE HOLD 18 FOOTBALL FANS IN DAWN RAIDS

A

POLICE investigating football violence ,arrested eighteen people yesterday in dawn raids on homes in London and the Home Counties.

Detectives said they hoped they had 'bro- ken the the back of a hard-core element' of violent football fans. Weapons including knives, coshes and a crossbow were seized by the ninety officers involved in the raids.

B

PROTESTING nurses mounted a mass demonstration at the House of Commons yesterday but were held back by a cordon of police, who used five riot control vans to stop the marchers entering Parliament Square.

Some nurses complained of rough treatment by the police. One male nurse claimed he had been hit on the shoulder with a truncheon and at least two nurses were arrested.

C

POLICE will use guns and appropriate force when dealing with armed criminals, Scotland Yard warned yesterday. The statement came after a judge sentenced a gang of five to a total of fifty-five years' jail for armed robbery.

'When faced with armed criminals, we will reply with appropriate force. Our duty remains to combat crime.'

Glossary
sentence (v) to give official punishment
raid (n) here, a sudden visit by the police looking for criminals or illegal goods
hard core element here, a violent group
crossbow a powerful weapon which combines a bow and a gun

VOCABULARY
Prepositions after verbs

Complete the sentences below with the correct preposition.

for   of   to   with   about   from

EXAMPLE
1 The police often have to deal . . . dangerous criminals.
  The police often have to deal with dangerous criminals.

2 The protesters were prevented . . . entering Parliament Square.
3 The children were warned . . . the dangers of drugs.
4 The criminal was sentenced . . . five years in prison.
5 She was accused . . . armed robbery.
6 The nurses complained . . . unnecessary police violence.
7 The demonstrators were arrested outside the US embassy . . . disturbing the peace.
8 Even on the beat, a police officer might be faced . . . a dangerous situation.

▣ LISTENING

1 Listen to a radio news report and note:
  what London Regional Transport are worried about.
  who is causing the trouble.

2 Listen again and note five measures which are being taken to try to solve the problem.

TALKING POINT

1 Should police be present at political demonstrations and sports events like football matches? Should they be armed?
2 Do violent TV programmes and films make police work more dangerous?

-46-

Grammar

Past perfect simple

Errol and his girlfriend, Judy, were very excited because Judy's father had managed to get them two tickets for the football Cup Final at Wembley Stadium. They caught an early train to London and spent the morning looking round the shops. They arrived at Wembley at two o'clock and joined the queue to get in. Imagine their horror at the turnstile when they realised they had left the tickets at home!

Put the events in the order in which they actually occurred.

1 Errol and Judy arrived at Wembley Stadium.
2 They left the tickets at home.
3 They spent the morning shopping.
4 Judy's father gave Errol and Judy two tickets for the Cup Final at Wembley.
5 They caught an early train to London.

What's the difference in meaning?

1 Errol was feeling pleased. He bought himself a new jacket.
2 Errol was feeling pleased. He had bought himself a new jacket.

Look at the Focus section and see if you can find the answer.

FOCUS

The past perfect

This tense is used

- To refer to something that happened before another action or state in the past:
  They were excited because Judy's father had managed to get them tickets for the match.

- To describe earlier events when telling a story in the past:
  What an awful day! Everything had gone wrong from the moment she woke up . . .

- In reported speech and thoughts:
  They realised they had forgotten the tickets.

PRACTICE

1 Join the sentences using *because* and the past perfect.

EXAMPLE
1 Judy and Errol spent the morning shopping. They were tired.
Judy and Errol were tired because they had spent the morning shopping.

2 He didn't work hard enough during the year. He failed his exam.
3 Mike left his wallet at home. He was cross.
4 They didn't pay their telephone bill. The telephone company cut them off.
5 They left their passports at home. They couldn't cross the frontier.
6 She lost her glasses. She couldn't read the sign.

2 Complete the following sentences using the past perfect.

1 When I went to pay, I realised that . . .
2 When he arrived at the station, he saw that . . .
3 When they got home, they found that . . .
4 Soon after the wedding, she knew that . . .
5 When I asked about the mess on the floor, she said that . . .

🖳 LISTENING

Listen to Errol's young brother, Michael, talking to a friend about something which happened to him recently.
1 Where was Michael going and why?
2 Why did he miss the ferry?

WRITING

Write Michael's story using the notes below to help you. Use the past perfect tense where necessary.

Michael/very excited/got job for skiing season in a resort in Austria. Good skier/skiied a lot at school. Went by train to Dover/and because arrived early/went to a café to get something to drink. Put backpack beside chair/while drinking tea. When went to catch midnight ferry/no ticket or passport/realised someone stolen them.

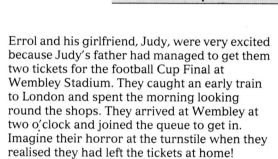

THE EVENING NEWS, Monday Dec. 6, 1926.

The Evening News

LARGEST EVENING NET SALE IN THE WORLD.

NO. 14,928.   FORTY-SIXTH YEAR.   LONDON: MONDAY, DECEMBER 6, 1926.   ONE PENNY.

HOME ED.

ASK FOR NICHOLSON'S GIN — THE PUREST SPIRIT MADE

THE MYSTERY OF AGATHA CHRISTIE.

MISSING NOVELIST UNTRACED.

PROMISE TO "COMMUNICATE" THAT WAS NOT KEPT.

COL. CHRISTIE'S JOURNEY.

SCOTLAND YARD UNABLE TO HELP UNTIL "CALLED IN."

ALTHOUGH the search has now spread over several counties, there is still no trace of Mrs. Agatha Clarissa Christie, the novelist-wife of Col. Archibald Christie, C.M.G., D.S.O., of The Styles, Sunningdale, Berkshire.

Since she left home on Friday night, saying that she was going for a motor drive, that she would not return home that night, and that she would "ring up" when she reached her destination, she has vanished completely.

Her car was found the next morning overhanging the lip of a chalk pit at Shere, Surrey. It had in it a fur coat—which she would certainly have taken in the bitterly cold weather if she had proceeded anywhere on foot—some other garments and an attaché case containing her driving license and unimportant papers.

HUSBAND WITHOUT NEWS.

Colonel Christie said to The Evening News to-day: "I can obtain no news whatever of my wife, nor can I suggest any reason why she should have left home, but she had lately been in a very bad nervous condition."

Colonel Christie motored to Scotland Yard to-day to enlist their help in the search, but was told that the "Yard" could not step in unless requested by the Guildford headquarters of the Surrey police. Mrs. Christie's description had, however, been circulated to all Metropolitan stations. The Colonel then went on to Guildford.

Mrs. Christie wrote detective stories with a strong vein of humour not usually associated with that type of fiction. Two—"Anne the Adventurous" and "Who Killed Ackroyd?"—appeared in serial form in The Evening News.

SEARCHERS IN THE MIST.

Police Difficulties in Lovely but Lonely Woods: Dragging the "Silent Pool" Again.

From Our Special Correspondent.

GUILDFORD, Monday.

MRS. AGATHA CHRISTIE has given the Surrey Constabulary as perplexing a problem as any in her detective novels by her mysterious disappearance near Newlands Corner, the famous beauty spot at Shere, on Friday night.

Deputy Chief Constable Kenward, of the Surrey Constabulary, personally took part in another systematic search through the woods and bracken and only tracks converging on the Corner. They had searched in vain throughout the whole day yesterday, starting from the spot where Mrs. Christie's abandoned car had been found in the undergrowth on the edge of a chalk pit.

SEARCHERS SOAKED BY DENSE MIST.

To assist him in the formidable task of not only searching the miles of bracken and undergrowth, but also in dragging the numerous pools, Mr. Kenward had obtained the help of scores of

TIME-TABLE OF THE MYSTERY.

p.m. Friday.—Mrs. Christie arrives at her home, The Styles, Sunningdale, Berks., from a tea-visit to friends at Dorking, and spends the evening with her husband.

p.m. Friday.—She packs into an attaché case a dress, some shoes and toilet articles and departs for her woman secretary that she is going for a drive and will not be back that night, but will communicate in the morning.

a.m. Saturday.—The car found wedged in a thick hedge at the lip of a chalk pit at Newlands Corner, Shere, Surrey, 15 miles from Sunningdale. In the car were a fur coat, grey jumper, a grey frock, two pairs of black shoes and the attaché case containing papers of no significance and Mrs. Christie's driving license.

"SHINGLED REDDISH HAIR."

Mrs. Christie's description as given by the police is as follows: Aged 35, height 5ft. 7in., reddish hair, shingled; grey eyes, fair complexion, and well built; wearing a grey stockinette skirt, green jumper, grey cardigan, and a small velour hat.

She had a platinum ring with one pearl, but no wedding ring; and a black handbag containing probably £5 to £10.

Pool. I found it overgrown with weeds, although the water is wonderfully clear.

On two sides of this pool there are sheer banks covered with thick undergrowth and although the police dragged this yesterday they intend to do so again later to-day.

Other pools they intend visiting and dragging include Albury Mill Pool, a large pool directly in front of the mill and very close to the old Wonersh Mill Pool and the Bramley Pool, which is a kind of wide stream about four miles away.

THE MOTOR-CAR EXPERT.

Among the party brought to-day by the deputy chief constable by car to Newlands Corner was a motor-car expert who examined carefully the steep hill from the corner to the chalk pit.

The police hold several theories. One is that Mrs. Christie may have become alarmed by her car suddenly starting at the top of the hill.

They have consulted the motor-car expert, and are inclined to believe that the car may have been in gear when she was starting it up and that it suddenly dashed into a very nervous temperament.

WIFE'S SECRET ADDRESS.

WRITTEN ON CARD FOR DIVORCE JUDGE.

THREATS BY 'PHONE.

THROUGH her counsel, the Hon. Victor Russell, Mrs. Elsie May Knight...

GODFREY TEARLE ILL.

REVIVAL OF "ALOMA" POSTPONED.

Owing to the illness of Mr. Godfrey Tearle, the revival of "Aloma," the South Sea romance, announced for to-night at the Adelphi, has had to be postponed. The Evening News was informed that he is suffering from tonsilitis, but is somewhat better to-day after a comfortable night.

His doctor has forbidden him to appear on the stage for the...

Agatha Christie (1891-1976) is one of the world's best-known and best-loved authors. Her famous detectives, Hercule Poirot and Miss Marple, and her brilliantly constructed plots have caught the imagination of generations of readers. Although she lived to an old age and wrote many books, she did not reveal much about her personal life.

In December 1926 an incident occurred which would have made an enthralling detective story in itself. At the height of her success with her first novel, she apparently vanished into thin air for ten days. At the time she was extremely distressed because she had found out that her husband was having an affair with another woman and wanted a divorce. She was sleeping badly, she couldn't write and she was eating very little.

On Friday 3rd December, Agatha told her secretary and companion, Carlo (Miss Charlotte Fisher), that she wanted a day alone. When Carlo returned in the evening, she found that the garage doors had been left open and the maids were looking frightened. According to them, Mrs Christie had come downstairs at about eleven in the evening, had got into her car and had driven off quickly without saying anything to anybody.

Carlo waited up anxiously all night but Agatha did not return. Early the next morning the police found Agatha's car in a ditch with its lights on. There was no trace of Agatha.

A nation-wide hunt for the missing novelist was started. The police were suspicious. Did the servants know something more? Was Agatha's husband hiding something? Newspapers printed wild stories about her disappearance — that she had committed suicide, that she had been kidnapped, that she had run away with a secret lover; some even suggested that she had planned the whole thing as a publicity stunt.

The mystery ended ten days later when Agatha was found alive and well in Harrogate, a health spa in Yorkshire. Her husband explained to the waiting reporters that she had lost her memory. But to this day, nobody really knows what happened during those missing ten days.

Glossary
publicity stunt an action to gain attention
health spa a resort with spring water where people come for health cures

Topic

Mysteries and thrillers

1 Read and answer.

1 When did Agatha disappear?
2 Why was she distressed at the time?
3 What did she tell her companion, Carlo?
4 What did Carlo find on her return?
5 What had happened at eleven o'clock according to the maids?
6 What did the police find?
7 What did the newspapers suggest had happened to Agatha?
8 Where and when did Agatha reappear?
9 What explanation did her husband give?

2 Guess the meaning

enthralling   vanished into thin air
distressed   ditch   trace   kidnap

3 Cover the text and use the questions and answers from Exercise 1 to retell the story of Agatha Christie's disappearance.

4 Read and think.

1 Do you think Agatha lost her memory?
2 What do you think happened during those ten days?
3 What effect do you think her disappearance had on her marriage after her return?

VOCABULARY

Match the type of book with a suitable title.

BOOK
a detective story
a biography
an autobiography
a thriller
a travel book
a romantic novel
a collection of short stories

TITLE
Long Lost Love
Fear Strikes at Midnight
'Tramp' and other stories
The life of Jane Austen
Mainly Me, Myself and I
Mystery at Highview House
In the steps of Marco Polo

TALKING POINT

Which of the following do you think makes a book a good thriller or detective story? Refer to any books which you have read or liked.

- short sentences and short chapters
- an exciting ending to each chapter
- an exotic location
- plenty of action
- a simple plot
- plenty of violent murders
- a likeable detective
- romantic interest
- a surprise ending
- authentic background detail

WRITING

Linking devices: contrast

As well as with *but* and *however,* you can express contrast using *although* and *in spite of.* *In spite of* is followed by a noun or a verb in the *-ing* form. It is used when the subject of both the sentences is the same.

EXAMPLE
Although Agatha Christie lived to an old age, the public knew little about her personal life.

In spite of living to an old age, Agatha Christie did not reveal much about her personal life.

1 Rewrite these sentences using *although* or *in spite of.*

1 Carlo suspected Agatha would not return but she waited up anxiously all night.
2 They searched everywhere but they did not find Mrs Christie.
3 Agatha Christie knew about her husband's affair with another woman but she still loved him.
4 Her husband said that she had lost her memory but nobody knows the truth.

2 Write two or three paragraphs about a murder mystery or thriller you have enjoyed reading or watching on TV.

Say where the story takes place and who the main characters are, and give a brief outline of the plot. Also say why you liked the book or film. Try to include a contrasting idea using *although* or *in spite of.*

Communication

Expressing regrets

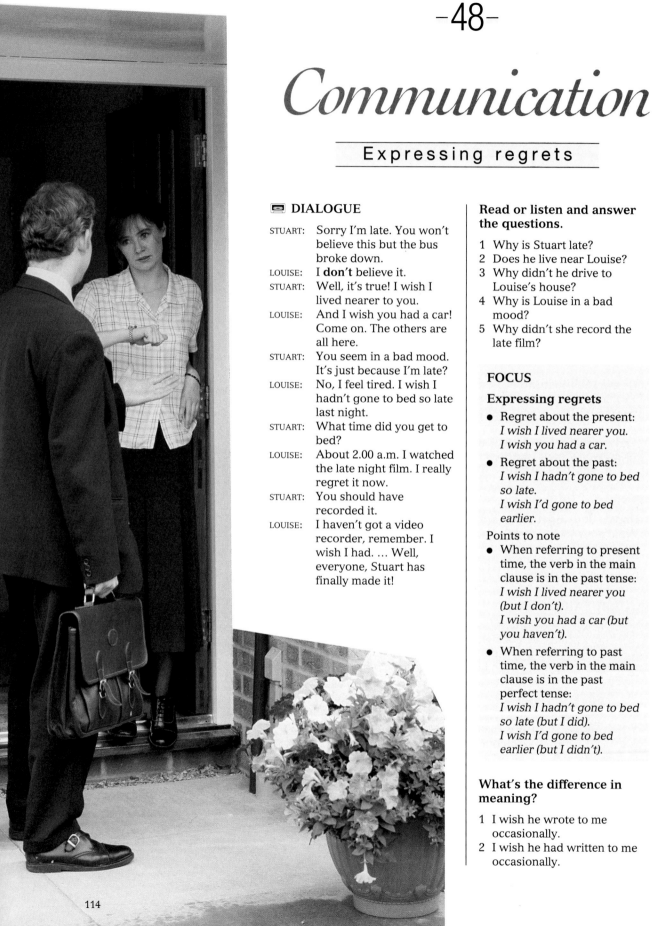

▣ DIALOGUE

STUART: Sorry I'm late. You won't believe this but the bus broke down.

LOUISE: I **don't** believe it.

STUART: Well, it's true! I wish I lived nearer to you.

LOUISE: And I wish you had a car! Come on. The others are all here.

STUART: You seem in a bad mood. It's just because I'm late?

LOUISE: No, I feel tired. I wish I hadn't gone to bed so late last night.

STUART: What time did you get to bed?

LOUISE: About 2.00 a.m. I watched the late night film. I really regret it now.

STUART: You should have recorded it.

LOUISE: I haven't got a video recorder, remember. I wish I had. … Well, everyone, Stuart has finally made it!

Read or listen and answer the questions.

1 Why is Stuart late?
2 Does he live near Louise?
3 Why didn't he drive to Louise's house?
4 Why is Louise in a bad mood?
5 Why didn't she record the late film?

FOCUS

Expressing regrets

● Regret about the present:
I wish I lived nearer you.
I wish you had a car.

● Regret about the past:
I wish I hadn't gone to bed so late.
I wish I'd gone to bed earlier.

Points to note

● When referring to present time, the verb in the main clause is in the past tense:
I wish I lived nearer you (but I don't).
I wish you had a car (but you haven't).

● When referring to past time, the verb in the main clause is in the past perfect tense:
I wish I hadn't gone to bed so late (but I did).
I wish I'd gone to bed earlier (but I didn't).

What's the difference in meaning?

1 I wish he wrote to me occasionally.
2 I wish he had written to me occasionally.

PRACTICE

1 Look at the example then complete the sentences in the same way.

EXAMPLE
1 I wish I lived nearer town . . .
   I wish I lived nearer town but I don't.

2 I wish I was good at tennis . . .
3 I wish I'd brought some warmer clothes . . .
4 I wish I hadn't lent her my bike . . .
5 I wish I didn't live in the country . . .
6 I wish I could speak German . . .

2 Work in pairs. Make a list of things you don't like about yourself and your present situation.

Think about your job, your studies, your friends and social life, your home life, your appearance, your abilities and your daily routine.

3 Now talk about your present life.

EXAMPLE   SOCIAL LIFE:
           I wish I had a car.

4 What things in your past life do you regret? Rewrite the regrets below as full sentences using *I wish* and the past perfect tense.

EXAMPLE
1 not working harder at school.
   I wish I'd worked harder at school

1 not working harder at school.
2 giving up piano lessons.
3 not reading more books.
4 not taking up acting.
5 not getting to know my grandparents better before they died.
6 not travelling when I had the opportunity.
7 going straight into work from school.
8 spending all my money on records and clothes.

📼 LISTENING

Listen to a young man talking about his university career. What does he regret about his education so far? Listen again and note the different ways in which he expresses these regrets. Expand the notes into sentences starting with: *He wishes he . . .*

WRITING

Write a simple short story starting with one of the following lines.
I wish I had never . . . bought the piano.
                       invited Carlos home.
                       put the advertisement in the paper.
                       decided to take riding lessons.
                       taken the short cut to work.

Start like this:
I wish I had never decided to take riding lessons. It all started like this . . .

TALKING POINT

Look at the pictures of the two public telephone boxes below.

Which is the older one? What are the differences between them? Why do you think some people wish they had kept the old type?

What changes in the name of 'progress' have been made in your town or area? How do you feel about them?

EXAMPLE
I wish they hadn't destroyed the old railway station.

I only parked here for a few minutes.

Yes, but you're on a double yellow line. If you'd parked on a meter, you wouldn't have got a ticket.

If there hadn't been a queue at the bank, I'd have got back before she caught me.

49

Grammar

Third conditional *if* clauses

Answer the questions.

1 Did the woman park on a meter?
2 Did the traffic warden give her a parking ticket?
3 Why didn't she get back earlier?

What's the difference in meaning?

1 If you parked on a meter, you wouldn't get a ticket.
2 If you'd parked on a meter, you wouldn't have got a ticket.

What does '*d* stand for in the second sentence? What differences are there in the verb tenses in these sentences?

FOCUS

The third (or past) conditional

This structure is used
- to imagine consequences of things that did not happen in the past:
  If you'd (had) parked on a meter, you wouldn't have got a ticket.
  (You didn't park on a meter so you got a ticket.)
  If there hadn't been a queue at the bank, I'd have (would have) got back before she caught me.

Points to note
- *Would have* never occurs in the *if* clause.

- *Might have* or *could have* are used instead of *would have* if the consequence is less definite:
  If you'd asked me earlier, I might have been able to help.

PRACTICE

1 Join each pair of sentences to make one sentence in the third conditional.

EXAMPLE

1 I borrowed the money.
I was able to buy the bike.

If I hadn't borrowed the money, I wouldn't have been able to buy the bike.

2 I didn't catch the bus.
I was late for work.
3 I watched the late-night film on television. I overslept.
4 I didn't work hard at school. I didn't get to university.
5 We couldn't find a baby-sitter. We didn't go out.
6 She went out with wet hair. She caught a cold.

2 Write new sentences using a third conditional and the words in brackets.

EXAMPLE

1 I'm glad you reminded me about Jack's birthday. (forget)

If you hadn't reminded me about Jack's birthday, I'd have forgotten about it.

2 If only I'd left earlier! (miss train)
3 I wish I'd taken more money with me. (buy that jacket)
4 Why did I eat so much last night! (feel so awful today)
5 It's a good thing that you were wearing seatbelts. (may get hurt)
6 Unfortunately the car broke down. (go to the party)

⊡ LISTENING

Listen to two people talking about an incident which happened recently in London involving a businessman and a taxi driver. Answer the questions.

1 What was the businessman carrying?
2 Where had he been?
3 Where did he get out of the taxi?
4 What did he discover and what did he do about it?
5 What did the taxi driver do?

TALKING POINT

1 What would you have done if you'd been the taxi driver?
2 How could the taxi driver have 'vanished into thin air'?
3 What would you have asked or said to the businessman if you'd been the policeman in charge of the incident?

Doctor saves man in Jet Drama

SIXTY-FIVE-YEAR-OLD Mr Ivan Kowalski had a lucky escape yesterday when he collapsed from lack of oxygen on a flight to Warsaw.

The British Airways Tristar en route to Warsaw had been flying steadily at 30,000 feet when it suddenly flew into a storm.

According to flight attendant Marie Parks: 'It was extremely bumpy. Even the crew had to strap themselves in.'

Mr Kowalski, who was on his way to visit relations in Poland, said: 'I felt a sudden pain in the chest and couldn't breathe. It was very frightening indeed. I was lucky there was a doctor on board.'

Said 43-year-old Canadian doctor, Peter Jenkins: 'I only did what any other doctor would do. It was a very turbulent flight.

The man had obviously panicked and the panic had brought on a bad attack of asthma. Fortunately there is always oxygen on board for this type of emergency.'

READING

1 Read the newspaper article and answer the questions.

1 Who had a lucky escape?
2 What happened and why?
3 Who helped him and how?

2 Complete the sentences using the information from the news item.

1 The flight wouldn't have been so bumpy if . . .
2 If Mr Kowalski hadn't panicked, . . .
3 Mr Kowalski might have died if . . .
4 The doctor wouldn't have been able to help him if . . .

WRITING

Either write a short news story with the headline: BOY SAVED IN DRAMATIC HELICOPTER RESCUE or write about another dramatic incident which might have had tragic consequences if certain actions had not been taken.

Use the text about Mr Kowalski as a guide for your writing. Say who was involved in the incident and where it took place. Say briefly what happened and end your news story with a sentence starting with If . . .

Reading

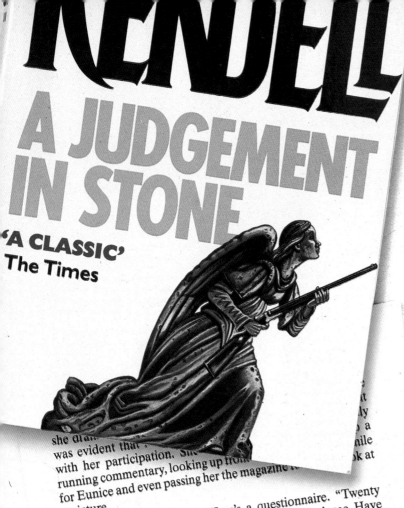

RENDELL

A JUDGEMENT IN STONE

'A CLASSIC'
The Times

she drank ... was evident that ... with her participation. She ... running commentary, looking up from ... for Eunice and even passing her the magazine ... a picture.

Melinda turned the page. 'Here's a questionnaire. "Twenty Questions to Test if You're Really in Love." Now let's see. Have you got a pencil or pen or something?'

A firm shake of the head from Eunice.

'I've got a pen in my bag,' Eunice, watching her fetch it, hoped she would take bag, pen and magazine elsewhere, but Melinda returned to her place at the table. 'Now, "Question One: Would you rather be with him than . . ." Oh I can see the answers at the bottom, that's no good, I'll tell you what, you ask me the questions and tick if I get three marks or two or none at all. O.K?'

'I haven't got my glasses,' said Eunice.

'Yes, you have. They're in your pocket.'

And they were. The tortoise-shell ones. The pair the Coverdales knew as her reading glasses. Eunice didn't put them on. She did nothing for she didn't know what to do. She couldn't say she was too busy. Too busy for what?

Melinda reached across and picked the glasses out of her pocket. Eunice made no move to take them. She was trying to think. What to do, how to get out of it. Puzzled, Melinda let her hand fall, and as she did so, she looked through the glasses from a short distance and saw that they were of plain glass. Her eyes went to Eunice's flushed face, her blank stare, and pieces of the puzzle — the way she never read a book, looked at a paper, left a note, got a letter — fell into place.

'Miss Parchman,' she said quietly, 'are you dyslexic?'

Vaguely, Eunice thought this must be the name of some eye disease.

'Pardon?' she said hopefully.

'I'm sorry, I mean you can't read, can you? You can't read or write.'

A JUDGEMENT IN STONE
by Ruth Rendell

If the Coverdales had not been so desperate for help, they would never have employed Eunice Parchman for the job as housekeeper. And if they hadn't been so kind to her, Eunice would never have hated them so much. And if they hadn't discovered her terrible secret, she might never have murdered them…

🔲 LISTENING

Listen to an extract from a radio programme about the latest crime books. The panel are discussing *A Judgement in Stone* by Ruth Rendell.

Note:
1 what Eunice's terrible secret was.
2 why the book is unusual.

The extract on the left from the novel describes how Eunice's secret is revealed to the daughter of the house.

Guess the meaning
puzzled   flushed   blank
vaguely   disease

COMPREHENSION
Answer the questions.

1 What did Melinda find in her magazine?
2 Why did Eunice give 'a firm shake of the head'?
3 What did Melinda want Eunice to do?
4 How did Eunice try to avoid doing it?
5 Was this true?
6 How did Melinda find out that Eunice's glasses weren't real?
7 What other clues made Melinda suspect that Eunice was dyslexic?

THINK ABOUT IT

1 Why did Eunice keep the glasses in her pocket?
2 Why do you think Eunice's face was flushed?

TALKING POINT

1 If you had been Eunice, how would you have avoided doing the questionnaire?
2 Imagine that you couldn't read or write. How would it affect your daily life? What sort of things would you be unable to do and enjoy?
3 What sort of help can be given to people who are dyslexic?

STYLE

Some of the sentences in the text are not complete sentences. They have no main verbs.

EXAMPLE
A firm shake of the head by Eunice.

This has the effect of making the narrative more dramatic. How many more examples of sentences without main verbs can you find? What are the missing parts of the sentence in each case?

VOCABULARY

An adverb is often used after the verb *said* to describe the way something is spoken.

EXAMPLE
'Miss Parchman,' she said quietly.

1 Write adverbs from the following adjectives.

nervous   suspicious   rude   angry   enthusiastic   hopeful

2 Now select the correct adverb to complete the following.

1 'I don't care who you are,' she said . . .
2 'Perhaps she'll be on the next train,' she said . . .
3 'Get out of here,' he said . . .
4 'Is it my turn now?' he asked . . .
5 'We've got a terrific timetable this term,' said the girl . . .
6 'What have you put in here?' she asked . . .

3 🖭 Adverb stress

Listen and repeat the adverbs. Notice where the main stress falls and write it in capital letters.

EXAMPLE
nervously   NERVously

WRITING

1 Rewrite the following two paragraphs from *A Judgement in Stone* inserting the correct punctuation and capital letters.

the silence endured for a full minute melinda too had blushed why didnt you tell us she said as eunice got up wed have understood lots of people are dyslexic i did a study of it in my last year at school Miss Parchman shall i teach you to read im sure it could be fun i could begin in the easter holidays

eunice took the two mugs and set them on the draining board she stood still with her back to melinda then she turned round slowly and fixed melinda with a stare if you tell anyone im what you said ill tell your dad youve been going with that boy and youre going to have a baby

2 In pairs or individually, use your imagination to write the next 200 words of the book.

Imagine what Melinda said in reply and how the dialogue continued. What do you think they did after they had finished talking?
Make sure you punctuate any dialogue correctly. Read your versions out to each other afterwards.

Check

♈ ♉ ♊ ♋ ♌ ♍ ♎ ♓ ♑ ♏ ♐ ♒

YOUR HANDS WILL REVEAL YOUR CHARACTER AND LIFE PATTERN.

DR. LINDSAY
D.M.S. ASTRAL

Your personal horoscope individually interpreted in detail.
Phone 0772 58623 for an appointment.

♑ ♒ ♓ ♎ ♈ ♉ ♊ ♋ ♌ ♍ ♐ ♏

1 You go to see Dr Lindsay. Report what he told you.

1 'One of your relatives is ill in hospital.'
2 'You have been worrying a lot lately.'
3 'A friend of yours has just had a baby.'
4 'You received an important letter last week.'
5 'You are going to travel abroad next summer.'
6 'You will meet and fall in love with a stranger.'
7 'I can see a wedding in your life.'
8 'You are improving at English.'

2 Report the questions you asked Dr Lindsay.

1 'What can you see in my palm?'
2 'What are my career chances?'
3 'How long am I going to live?'
4 'Have I got any hidden health problem?'
5 'Where will I be next year?'
6 'When am I going to get married?'
7 'Did I pass my exam yesterday?'
8 'Are my parents going to move house?'

3 Choose from the verbs of reporting below to complete the sentences.

invite   refuse   suggest   promise   remind   tell   warn

1 'Tomorrow's class is cancelled.'
   (The teacher/us)
2 'Would you like to come to the café with us?'
   (She/me)
3 'I can't let you into the match without a ticket.'
   (The man/them)
4 'I'll phone this evening. Don't worry.' (She . . .)
5 'Don't forget to double-lock the front door.'
   (The caretaker/them)
6 'Let's buy her a bunch of white roses.' (He . . .)
7 'I wouldn't cycle on the main road if I were you.'
   (She/him)

4 Imagine you are a young person in a boring job. Write regrets about your present situation starting with *I wish*.

1 'I don't like my job'.
2 'I have to get up so early.'
3 'I don't earn very much money.'
4 'I'm not interested in a career.'
5 'I haven't got anywhere to live.'
6 'I don't know what I want to do with my life.'

5 Write regrets about your recent visit to Britain, starting with *I wish*.

1 'I didn't go to Scotland.'
2 'I didn't know about the Edinburgh festival.'
3 'I didn't have time to see a typical English village.'
4 'I stayed with our group all the time.'
5 'I didn't take my camera.'
6 'I didn't manage to get a ticket to see "Phantom of the Opera."'

6 Match the two halves of the sentences.

1 They would have got better exam results
2 She would have gone to California
3 If you'd told me the date of her birthday
4 I would have bought a new suit
5 If I hadn't missed the turning
6 If I'd known about her accident
7 If you'd warned me about the mosquitos
8 The house might have caught fire

a) if I'd known about the sale.
b) I wouldn't have got lost.
c) I would have visited her in hospital.
d) I wouldn't have camped by the lake.
e) if she hadn't smelt burning.
f) if she'd got that American job.
g) if they'd studied a bit harder.
h) I would have sent her a card.

7 Read the following situations and write sentences with *if*.

1 I didn't know you needed the eggs for the cake. I used them all.
2 She went to Mexico. She met her future husband.
3 You didn't take my advice. You lost your wallet.
4 He didn't send off the form in time. He didn't get a prize.
5 She hurt her ankle. She didn't win the match.
6 It was foggy. I arrived late.
7 You told me the ending. I didn't enjoy the film.
8 I didn't know the time of your train. I couldn't meet you at the station.
9 The fire didn't spread. There wasn't much wind.
10 I cleared out my handbag. I lost your telephone number.

8 Choose the correct response.

1 A: Good luck on Monday!
   B: a) Yes, I will.
       b) And to yours.
       c) Thanks a lot.

2 A: Bye bye, and don't get sunburnt.
   B: a) Thanks, I'll need it.
       b) Don't worry, I won't.
       c) The same to you.

3 A: Have a nice weekend!
   B: a) Thanks and the same to you.
       b) Don't worry, I won't.
       c) I really must be going.

4 A: Give my regards to your family.
   B: a) No, I won't.
       b) Thanks, I will.
       c) Goodbye.

9 What would you say in the following situations?

1 A colleague indicates that she wants to speak to you while you are talking to someone on the phone.
2 Your doorbell rings while you are in the middle of a telephone conversation with a friend.
3 You meet an ex-colleague from work in the street during your lunch hour. You would like to meet them again.
4 You say goodbye to some friends who are going on holiday.

Use your English

1 In pairs, rearrange the paragraphs in the correct order to form a newspaper article under the heading 'Pupils in Terror Ride'.

EXAMPLE
1c 2 …

a) Said Mrs Ann Stoker, whose children, Caroline, fourteen, and Tom, sixteen, were on the bus: 'Anything could have happened. I don't care how naughty the children were. It was quite wrong to drop them thirty miles away from home.'

b) They said that he suddenly slammed the doors shut and accelerated so fast that some of the children had fallen and hit their heads.

c) The driver of a double decker school bus was being questioned by police yesterday after parents had complained that he had taken twenty of their children on a high-speed terror ride and left them locked in the bus thirty miles from home.

d) A spokesman for the bus company said: 'We are looking into the matter. The driver was clearly provoked.'

e) Anxious parents telephoned the bus company and the school when their children failed to return at the usual time.

f) Eventually a handful of 16-year-olds managed to break out of the bus and telephone their parents. They said that the driver had got angry because some of them had been running up and down the stairs ringing the bell and shouting.

2 (Student B: page 128)
In Part 1 you have a list of half completed conditional sentences. In Part 2 you have a list of possible endings for Student B's sentences. You read your first sentence and Student B must choose a suitable ending from his/her list using the correct form of the verb. Then Student B reads one of his/her sentences for you to complete.

EXAMPLE
A: If the weather had been better, we …
B: … would have gone on a picnic.
B: If you'd looked both ways before crossing the road, you …

Part 1 (uncompleted sentences)
If the weather had been better …
If your birthday had fallen on a Saturday …
If I hadn't eaten so much last night …
I would have been on time if …
I wouldn't have spent so long on the phone if …

Part 2 (possible endings for Student B's sentences)
take you out for the evening
eat any more
phone me earlier
see the lorry
buy a couple of tickets

3 In pairs, complete the poem by choosing a word or phrase from the list. You need not use all the words, and you may use some of them more than once if you wish. Then read your version to the rest of the class.

smiled   cried   asked   looked   died   wanted
kissed   laughed   written a poem   kissed her hand
carried her bag

If she had … me
I would have …
If she had … at me
I would have … for her
If she had … me to
I would have …
If she had …
I would have …
and/but if she had … at me
I would have …

Progress test

GRAMMAR

1 Choose the correct answer.

1 He said he *has/had* already seen the film.
2 The policeman asked the woman what *her name was/was her name*.
3 The guard said that the train *had already left/already left*.
4 Goodbye! *I give/I'll give* you a ring some time.
5 She explained *me/to me* that she wasn't feeling very well.
6 The man warned us *to not touch/not to touch* the electric fence.
7 The woman offered *me/to me* a coffee.
8 Gerry persuaded *that she stay/her to stay*.
9 I suggested *to sit/sitting* nearer the front of the cinema.
10 When I got home I realised that I *lost/had lost* my keys.
11 I wish I *hadn't gone/didn't go* to bed so late last night.
12 If you *had stood/would have stood* closer, you would have got a better picture.

2 Correct the sentences.

1 She asked if he ever gets nervous.
2 I really must to go now.
3 Good luck for the exam.
4 Thanks and same to you.
5 He apologised that he was late.
6 She reminded to me about Sam's birthday next week.
7 We were prevented to go in the main square.
8 They were accused with entering the country illegally.

VOCABULARY

3 Choose the correct word.

1 The man was arrested for armed ... .
   a) theft   b) robbery   c) stealing
2 I'm not looking for anything special. Just an ... teapot.
   a) common   b) usual   c) ordinary
3 I asked him if he was ever ... of the dangers involved.
   a) conscious   b) conscientious   c) conscience
4 Her teacher ... her to do some more work.
   a) suggested   b) recommended   c) advised
5 ... me to take those books back to the library tomorrow.
   a) Remember   b) Remind   c) Recall
6 Have they been ... of any other crimes?
   a) accused   b) arrested   c) sentenced
7 They suddenly realised that they had ... the tickets at home.
   a) forgotten   b) left   c) remained
8 The story had a happy ... .
   a) end   b) finish   c) ending
9 She was suffering ... from overwork.
   a) in time   b) at the time   c) on time
10 I ... some money off my mother but I've already paid it back.
   a) took   b) lent   c) borrowed

USAGE

4 Complete each of the numbered gaps in the text from the list below.

has   station   series   employ   recent   advised   on   carry   summer   now   bring   students

Oxford has decided it ...(1)... had enough of attacks ...(2)... visiting language students. The city's police force will ...(3)... extra street patrols this ...(4)... in an attempt to ...(5)... to an end a ...(6)... of ugly incidents. Foreign ...(7)... are being encouraged to ...(8)... personal attack alarms. They are also being ...(9)... on general safety, cycling, queuing and obstruction. The decision follows a ...(10)... incident when two students were attacked outside the railway ...(11)... . The students were forced to hand over £4,000 and are ...(12)... said to be penniless.

Vocabulary list

This list contains all the words in the *Guess the meaning, Words to learn* and *Vocabulary* sections of the Students' Book. Pronunciation is shown in the system used in the *Longman Dictionary of Contemporary English*. The number following each word indicates the unit in which it first appears.

A

ability /əˈbɪlɪti/ **37**
able (v) /ˈeɪbəl/ **37**
act (of a play) (n) /ækt/ **25**
actor /ˈæktəʳ/ **25**
adore /əˈdɔːʳ/ **30**
affectionate /əˈfekʃənɪt/ **30**
aggressive /əˈgresɪv/ **31**
alien /ˈeɪliən/ **30**
although /ɔːlˈðəʊ/ **31**
amazing /əˈmeɪzɪŋ/ **20**
angry /æŋgri/ **50**
appalled /əˈpɔːld/ **15**
applaud (v) /əˈplɔːd/ **20**
appreciative /əˈpriːʃətɪv/ **20**
armchair /ˈɑːmtʃeəʳ/ **10**
aromatic /ˌærəˈmætɪk/ **30**
at all costs /ət ɔːl kɒsts/ **17**
athletics /æθˈletɪks/ **17**
attic /ˈætɪk/ **7**
audience /ˈɔːdiəns/ **25**
autobiography /ˌɔːtəbaɪˈɒgrəfi/ **47**
awful /ˈɔːfəl/ **7**

B

beat (v) /biːt/ **20**
beautiful /ˈbjuːtɪfəl/ **7**
biography /baɪˈɒgrəfi/ **47**
blank /blæŋk/ **50**
block (v) /blɒk/ **27**
block of flats /blɒk əv ˈflæts/ **27**
boarding school /ˈbɔːdɪŋ ˌskuːl/ **1**
bookcase /ˈbʊk-keɪs/ **10**
borough /ˈbʌrə/ **31**
bothered (to be) /ˈbɒðəʳd (tə bi)/ **1**
bow (v) /baʊ/ **25**
box (in a theatre) /bɒks/ **25**
boxing /ˈbɒksɪŋ/ **17**
box-office /bɒks ˈɒfɪs/ **25**
bracelet /ˈbreɪslɪt/ **31**
brave /breɪv/ **5**
brilliant /ˈbrɪljənt/ **37**
bring up /brɪŋ ˈʌp/ **11**
brooch /brəʊtʃ/ **31**
bully /ˈbʊli/ **5**
bungalow /ˈbʌŋgələʊ/ **27**
burglar /ˈbɜːgləʳ/ **41**
burglary /ˈbɜːgləri/ **41**
bursting out /ˌbɜːstɪŋ aʊt/ **10**

C

candle /ˈkændl/ **10**
candlestick /ˈkændl ˌstɪk/ **10**
cap (n) /kæp/ **15**
capability /ˌkeɪpəˈbɪlɪti/ **37**
care /keəʳ/ **30**
careless /ˈkeələs/ **30**
chapter /ˈtʃæptəʳ/ **25**
chase (v) /tʃeɪs/ **14**
cheat (v) /tʃiːt/ **17**
chest of drawers /tʃest əv drɔːz/ **20**
circle (of a theatre) /ˈsɜːkəl/ **25**
claim /kleɪm/ **1**
cluster (n) /ˈklʌstəʳ/ **15**
comedy /ˈkɒmɪdi/ **25**
commentary /ˈkɒməntəri/ **25**
competitive /kəmˈpetɪtɪv/ **17**
complicated /ˈkɒmplɪkeɪtɪd/ **30**
confess /kənˈfes/ **17**
conformist /kənˈfɔːmɪst/ **5**
conspirator /kənˈspɪrətəʳ/ **25**
conspire /kənˈspaɪəʳ/ **17**
constantly /ˈkɒnstəntli/ **31**
contradict /ˌkɒntrəˈdɪkt/ **30**
costume /ˈkɒstjʊm/ **7**
cottage /ˈkɒtɪdʒ/ **27**
cough /kɒf/ **31**
courier /ˈkʊriəʳ/ **11**
course (golf) /kɔːs/ **17**
court (tennis) (n) /kɔːt/ **17**
crack (v) /kræk/ **15**
crackle /ˈkrækəl/ **10**
crawling /ˈkrɔːlɪŋ/ **21**
crime /kraɪm/ **41**
criminal (n) /ˈkrɪmɪnəl/ **41**
cruel /ˈkruːəl/ **30**
cry (v) /kraɪ/ **20**
cuff-links /ˈkʌf lɪŋks/ **31**
curtain (in a theatre) /ˈkɜːtn/ **25**
curtain call /ˈkɜːtn kɔːl/ **25**

D

dagger /ˈdægəʳ/ **25**
daunting /ˈdɔːntɪŋ/ **35**
day school /ˈdeɪ ˌskuːl/ **1**
decide /dɪˈsaɪd/ **37**
decision /dɪˈsɪʒən/ **37**
degree /dɪˈgriː/ **1**
deliver /dɪˈlɪvəʳ/ **11**

demonstration /ˌdemənˈstreɪʃən/ **41**
detached house /dɪˈtætʃt ˈhaʊs/ **27**
detective story /dɪˈtektɪv ˌstɔːri/ **47**
develop /dɪˈveləp/ **11**
dilemma /dɪˈlemə/ **37**
director (of a play) /dɪˈrektəʳ/ **7**
discouraging /dɪsˈkʌrɪdʒɪŋ/ **35**
disease /dɪˈziːz/ **50**
distraction /dɪˈstrækʃən/ **25**
district /ˈdɪstrɪkt/ **27**
do someone a favour /duː ˌsʌmwʌn ə ˈfeɪvəʳ/ **21**
dreadful /ˈdredfəl/ **7**
dress code /dres kəʊd/ **35**
dressing room /ˈdresɪŋ ruːm/ **7**

E

ear (a good ...) /ɪəʳ/ **7**
earrings /ˈɪəˌrɪŋz/ **31**
emergency /ɪˈmɜːdʒənsi/ **41**
eminent /ˈemɪnənt/ **30**
energy /ˈenədʒi/ **23**
enough /ɪˈnʌf/ **31**
enthusiastic /ɪnˌθjuːziˈæstɪk/ **50**
entire /ɪnˈtaɪəʳ/ **20**
essential /ɪˈsenʃəl/ **37**
ethical /ˈeθɪkəl/ **37**
evening class /ˈiːvnɪŋ ˌklɑːs/ **1**
exaggerated /ɪgˈzædʒəreɪtɪd/ **35**
exclusive /ɪkˈskluːsɪv/ **17**
exhausted /ɪgˈzɔːstɪd/ **41**
exhibitionist /ˌeksɪˈbɪʃənɪst/ **35**
experiment /ɪkˈsperɪmənt/ **30**
extrovert /ˈekstrəvɜːt/ **5**

F

fail (an exam) /feɪl/ **1**
fake (adj) /feɪk/ **35**
fan (football) /fæn/ **20**
fanatic /fəˈnætɪc/ **11**
fascinate /ˈfæsɪneɪt/ **31**
finally /ˈfaɪnəli/ **21**
financial /fɪˈnænʃəl/ **31**
fine (v) /faɪn/ **17**
fireguard /ˈfaɪəgɑːd/ **10**

fireplace /ˈfaɪəpleɪs/ **10**
fixation /fɪkˈseɪʃən/ **20**
floodlit /ˈflʌdlɪt/ **27**
flourish (v) /ˈflʌrɪʃ/ **35**
flushed /flʌʃt/ **50**
football /ˈfʊtbɔːl/ **17**
footlights /ˈfʊtlaɪts/ **25**
foyer /ˈfɔɪeɪ/ **25**
free kick /friː kɪk/ **20**
funny /ˈfʌni/ **30**

G

get (a pass/good grade/degree) /get/ **1**
get into college /ˌget ɪntə ˈkɒlɪdʒ/ **1**
glamorous /ˈglæmərəs/ **7**
golf /gɒlf/ **17**
gold chain /gəʊld ˈtʃeɪn/ **31**
go to college /ˌgəʊ tə ˈkɒlɪdʒ/ **1**
go up /gəʊ ˈʌp/ **11**
grade /greɪd/ **1**
graduate (v) /ˈgrædʒueɪt/ **7**
grandly /grændli/ **25**
grin (n) /grɪn/ **41**
ground (football) /graʊnd/ **20**
guilty /ˈgɪlti/ **20**
gymnastics /dʒɪmˈnæstɪks/ **17**

H

half-hearted /ˌhɑːf ˈhɑːtɪd/ **37**
handle /ˈhændl/ **37**
hard /hɑːd/ **5**
hardworking /ˌhɑːdˈwɜːkɪŋ/ **5**
head (v) (a ball) /hed/ **20**
heart /hɑːt/ **30**
heartless /ˈhɑːtləs/ **30**
helpful /ˈhelpfəl/ **7**
home /həʊm/ **30**
homeless /ˈhəʊmləs/ **30**
hopeful /ˈhəʊpfəl/ **7**
house /haʊs/ **27**
hurricane /ˈhʌrɪkən/ **30**
hut /hʌt/ **27**

I

ice rink /ˈaɪs rɪŋk/ **17**
ice skating /ˈaɪs ˌskeɪtɪŋ/ **17**
immensely /ɪˈmensli/ **7**
important /ɪmˈpɔːtənt/ **37**
impress /ɪmˈpres/ **1**
independence /ˌɪndəˈpendəns/ **31**

instantly /'ɪnstəntli/ **27**
iron bar /'aɪən 'bɑːʳ/ **17**

J

job /dʒɒb/ **30**
jobless /'dʒɒbləs/ **30**

K

kick (v) /kɪk/ **20**

L

leap (v) /liːp/ **7**

M

mark (v) /mɑːk/ **1**
mantlepiece /'mæntlpiːs/ **10**
matting /'mætɪŋ/ **10**
medal /'medl/ **17**
motor racing /'məʊtə ˌreɪsɪŋ/ **17**
mugging /'mʌgɪŋ/ **41**
murder (v) /'mɜːdəʳ/ **41**
musical (n) /'mjuːzɪkəl/ **25**
mutter /'mʌtəʳ/ **15**
mysterious /mɪ'stɪəriəs/ **20**

N

necklace /'neklɪs/ **31**
nervous /'nɜːvəs/ **50**
noisy /'nɔɪzi/ **5**
nought /nɔːt/ **31**

O

obsession /əb'seʃən/ **20**
obviously /'ɒbvɪəsli/ **20**
offstage /ɒf steɪdʒ/ **25**
off duty /ɒf 'djuːti/ **41**
office block /'ɒfɪs ˌblɒk/ **27**
old-fashioned /ˌəʊld 'fæʃənd/ **30**
one-bedroom flat /'wʌn bedrʊm 'flæt/ **27**
orchestra /'ɔːkɪstrə/ **25**
outstanding /aʊt'stændɪŋ/ **37**
overestimate /ˌəʊvər'estɪmeɪt/ **35**

P

package /'pækɪdʒ/ **11**
pain /peɪn/ **30**
painless /'peɪnləs/ **30**
palace /'pælɪs/ **27**
pass (an exam) /pɑːs/ **1**
pass (n) /pɑːs/ **1**
parlour /'pɑːləʳ/ **20**
path /pɑːθ/ **15**
patrol (n) /pə'trəʊl/ **41**
peak /piːk/ **15**
penalty /'penlti/ **20**
pendant /'pendənt/ **31**
perceptive /pə'septɪv/ **30**
perfectly /pə'fɪktli/ **20**
persecute /'pɜːsɪkjuːt/ **21**
pickpocketing /'pɪkˌpɒkɪtɪŋ/ **41**

piles /paɪlz/ **10**
pitch (football) (n) /pɪtʃ/ **17/20**
play (n) /pleɪ/ **7**
player /'pleɪəʳ/ **20**
plump /plʌmp/ **15**
pool /puːl/ **17**
portrait /'pɔːtrət/ **25**
possibility /ˌpɒsɪ'bɪlɪti/ **37**
potentially /pə'tenʃəli/ **35**
pour /pɔːr/ **20**
power /'paʊəʳ/ **27**
praise (v) /preɪz/ **20**
prevent /prɪ'vent/ **27**
primary school /'praɪməri ˌskuːl/ **1**
prison sentence /'prɪzən 'sentəns/ **17**
private school /'praɪvɪt ˌskuːl/ **1**
privilege /'prɪvɪlɪdʒ/ **25**
probability /ˌprɒbə'bɪlɪti/ **37**
producer (of a play) /prə'djuːsəʳ/ **25**
protect /prə'tekt/ **37**
puzzled /'pʌzəld/ **50**

Q

qualification /ˌkwɒlɪfɪkeɪʃən/ **37**
quarrel (n) /'kwɒrəl/ **15**

R

raise /reɪz/ **7**
rape /reɪp/ **41**
rebel (n) /'rebəl/ **5**
receive /rɪ'siːv/ **25**
recommend /ˌrekə'mend/ **37**
recommendation /ˌrekəmen'deɪʃən/ **37**
reduce /rɪ'djuːs/ **5**
refreshing /rɪ'freʃɪŋ/ **30**
reservation /ˌrezə'veɪʃən/ **37**
resign from /rɪ'zaɪn frəm/ **17**
revise /rɪ'vaɪz/ **1**
rink /rɪŋk/ **17**
ring /rɪŋ/ **17/31**
riot /raɪət/ **41**
rise (n) /raɪz/ **11**
rival (n) /'raɪvəl/ **17**
robbery /'rɒbəri/ **41**
romantic novel /rəʊ'mæntɪk 'nɒvəl/ **47**
root /ruːt/ **7**
rough /rʌf/ **31**
rude /ruːd/ **30**
ruin (v) /'ruːɪn/ **15**

S

scandal /'skændl/ **17**
scene /siːn/ **25**
scenery /'siːnəri/ **7**
score (v) /skɔːʳ/ **20**

scrambling /'skræmblɪŋ/ **17**
scrape /skreɪp/ **27**
scratch (v) /skrætʃ/ **15**
secondary school /'sekəndri ˌskuːl/ **1**
semi-detached house /ˌsemidɪ'tætʃt 'haʊs/ **27**
sensible /'sensəbəl/ **7**
shame (n) /ʃeɪm/ **17**
shape /ʃeɪp/ **30**
shapeless /'ʃeɪpləs/ **10/30**
shoot (at a goal) /ʃuːt/ **20**
shoplifting /'ʃɒpˌlɪftɪŋ/ **41**
short stories /ˌʃɔːt 'stɔːriz/ **47**
shout (v) /ʃaʊt/ **1**
show off /ʃəʊ ɒf/ **35**
shrill /ʃrɪl/ **15**
silly /'sɪli/ **30**
skating /'skeɪtɪŋ/ **17**
skiing /'skiːɪŋ/ **17**
skyscraper /'skaɪˌskreɪpəʳ/ **27**
slope /sləʊp/ **17**
sloppy /'slɒpi/ **35**
soak /səʊk/ **15**
sober /'səʊbəʳ/ **35**
smuggling /'smʌglɪŋ/ **41**
spectacular /spek'tækʊələʳ/ **20**
spirit /'spɪrɪt/ **17**
spoil /spɔɪl/ **15/30**
spotlights /spɒt laɪts/ **25**
stadium /'steɪdiəm/ **20**
stage (of a theatre) /steɪdʒ/ **25**
stain (v) /steɪn/ **15**
stalls /stɔːlz/ **25**
stand (n) /stænd/ **20**
stand up for himself /stænd ʌp fə hɪm'self/ **5**
star (v) /stɑːʳ/ **7**
stare (at) /steəʳ/ **20**
startle /'stɑːtl/ **20**
state school /'steɪt skuːl/ **1**
steadily /'stedɪli/ **20**
stereotypical /steriəʊ'tɪpɪkəl/ **30**
storm (n) /stɔːm/ **21**
strong /strɒŋ/ **5/37**
succession (in quick) /sək'seʃən/ **7**
suffer /'sʌfəʳ/ **5**
suitable /'suːtəbəl/ **11**
superb /suː'pɜːb/ **20** B
superficial /ˌsuːpə'fɪʃəl/ **30**
suspicious /sə'spɪʃəs/ **50**
swimming /'swɪmɪŋ/ **17**
symbol /'sɪmbəl/ **27**

T

tablecloth /'teɪbəlˌklɒθ/ **10**
table tennis /'teɪbəl ˌtenɪs/ **17**
take (an exam) /teɪk/ **1**

take to extremes /teɪk tə ɪk'striːms/ **17**
talented /'tæləntɪd/ **1**
tall /tɔːl/ **5**
tangle (n) /'tæŋgəl/ **15**
team /tiːm/ **20**
tear (v) /teəʳ/ **15**
tease /tiːz/ **5**
tennis /'tenɪs/ **17**
terraced house /ˌterɪst 'haʊs/ **27**
terrific /tə'rɪfɪk/ **37**
theft /θeft/ **41**
though /ðəʊ/ **31**
thought /θɔːt/ **30**
thoughtless /'θɔːtləs/ **30**
thriller /'θrɪləʳ/ **47**
through /θruː/ **31**
tired /'taɪəd/ **37**
tough /tʌf/ **7/31**
track /træk/ **17**
track (running) (n) /træk/ **17**
traffic jam /'træfɪk ˌdʒæm/ **11**
tragedy /'trædʒɪdi/ **25**
transform /træns'fɔːm/ **30**
travel book /'trævəl bʊk/ **47**
trip (v) /trɪp/ **17**
trod (tread) /trɒd/ **10**
truck /trʌk/ **20**
true /truː/ **30**
truly /'truːli/ **20**
tunnel (n) /'tʌnl/ **20**
turn out to be /tɜːn aʊt tə biː/ **35**

U

undermine /ˌʌndə'maɪn/ **25**
under pressure /ˌʌndəʳ 'preʃəʳ/ **5**
uneven /ʌn'iːvən/ **20**
unscrupulous /ʌn'skruːpjʊləs/ **31**
use /juːz/ **30**
useless /'juːsləs/ **30**

V

vaguely /'veɪgli/ **50**
vampire /'væmpaɪəʳ/ **7**
victim /'vɪktɪm/ **7**
volleyball /'vɒlibɔːl/ **17**

W

walk-on /'wɔːk ɒn/ **25**
warehouse /'weəˌhaʊs/ **27**
washbasin /'wɒʃˌbeɪsən/ **10**
windowsill /'wɪndəʊˌsɪl/ **10**
witty /'wɪti/ **30**
wonderful /'wʌndəfəl/ **7**
wrestling /'resəlɪŋ/ **17**

X

xenophobic /ˌzenə'fəʊbɪk/ **30**

Student B material

Use your English Units 1–10

1 Student A has a picture of a party which is similar to yours. Listen carefully to Student A's description of what the people are doing and wearing and find eight differences between the two scenes.

2 Student A is going to read you some sentences and you must complete them by choosing the best ending from the sentences 1–4 below. Wait for Student A to speak first.

1 ... I was lying in the bath.
2 ... a carton of milk fell out onto the kitchen floor.
3 ... my mother phoned just as I was leaving.
4 ... my jeans got caught in the bicycle chain.

Now you start and ask Student A to complete your sentences.

5 While I was washing my hair this morning, ...
6 A student got up and started shouting while ...
7 The audience were laughing and enjoying themselves when suddenly ...
8 When I asked him who he was, ...

Use your English Units 11–20

1 You and Student A both have a list of offers and a list of plans. Student A starts by reading out his/her first plan and you must choose an appropriate offer from your list.

EXAMPLE
A: I'm going to give a party on Saturday.
B: I'll help you with the food.

Take it in turns to read out your plans. Student A starts.

Plans
paint my bedroom a different colour
do the washing up
catch the six o'clock bus
learn Italian this year
buy a second-hand bicycle

Offers (for Student A's plans)
bring over some CDs and join you
lay the table
help you with the food
lend you my book called *Summer Jobs*
come with you to see it

Use your English

Units 21–30

2 There are a number of missing words in your reading text (2, 4, 6, 8 and 10). Student A has the same text but with different missing words (1, 3, 5, 7 and 9). Complete your texts by asking each other in turn for the missing information, using the question word in brackets. Student A starts.

EXAMPLE

A: (1) What was the man called?

B: He was called Sir Guy Fawkes.

B: (2) Who did he plot to blow up?

Guy Fawkes Day

In 1606 in London, a man called Sir Guy Fawkes plotted to blow up ... (2 Who?) and the Houses of Parliament. The plot, called 'The Gunpowder Plot', was discovered on ... (4 When?). Guy Fawkes and his friends were executed on 5th November. Since then, every 5th November, people let off ... (6 What?), light bonfires and burn a ... (8 What?) – a life-size dummy which represents Guy Fawkes. Some people have bonfire parties in their gardens but nowadays a ... (10 What?) is organised in most towns and villages.

3 You are a customer with a number of complaints and Student A is an assistant in a department store. Look at the pictures and say what the matter is when Student A asks what's wrong.

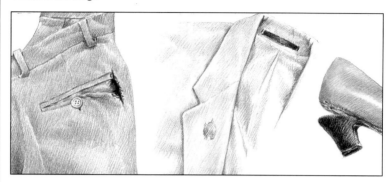

EXAMPLE

A: Is there anything wrong with your trousers?

B: Yes, I'm afraid the pocket is torn.

A: Oh, I'm sorry. I'll change them for another pair.

Now it is Student A's turn to be the customer. This time you are a waiter in a restaurant. Look at the pictures below and ask Student A what is wrong each time.

EXAMPLE

B: Is there anything wrong with your salad?

A: Yes, I'm afraid there's a caterpillar in it.

B: Oh, I'm sorry. I'll remove the salad immediately.

Offer to change the item of food each time.

Use your English Units 31–40

2 In Part 1 you have a list of half completed conditional sentences. In Part 2 you have a list of possible endings for Student A's sentences. Student A starts by reading his/her first sentence and you must choose a suitable ending from your list, choosing the correct form of the verb. Then it's your turn to read one of your sentences for Student A to complete.

EXAMPLE
A: If I got £100 for my birthday, …
B: I'd spend it on a pair of roller blades.
B: If I could go anywhere in the world …

Part 1 (uncompleted sentences)
If I could go anywhere in the world, I …
If a fire broke out in my house now, I …
If I got tickets for the Cup Final, would you …
Would you marry me if I …
My father would be very angry if he …
I would offer to help you if I …

Part 2 (possible endings for Student A's sentences)
pay me £50.
spend it on a pair of roller blades.
have the chance?
tell the store manager.
win a prize.
not mind very much.

3 Answer Student A's questions about the jobs which Stuart likes to do himself and those which he likes to have done. Then complete the information in your chart by asking Student A about Ruth. Student A starts.

EXAMPLE
A: What does Stuart do about servicing his car?
B: He usually has it serviced.

JOBS	Ruth		Stuart	
	HERSELF	SOMEONE ELSE	HIMSELF	SOMEONE ELSE
service the car				✓
alter his/her clothes				✓
type his/her letters			✓	
cut his/her hair				✓
decorate the house			✓	
clean the house				✓

Use your English
Units 41–50

2 In Part 1 you have a list of half completed conditional sentences. In Part 2 you have a list of possible endings for Student A's sentences. Student A starts by reading his/her first sentences and you must choose a suitable ending from your list, choosing the correct form of the verb. Then it's your turn to read one of your sentences for Student A to complete.

EXAMPLE
A: If the weather had been better, …
B: … we would have gone on a picnic.
B: If you'd looked both ways before crossing the road, you …

Part 1 (uncompleted sentences)
If you'd looked both ways before crossing the road …
If I hadn't spent all my money …
If the film had been worth seeing …
I wouldn't have got so worried if …
I would have been sick …

Part 2 (possible endings for Student A's sentences)
sleep better
go on a picnic
not lose my keys as I was leaving
know you wanted to make a call
take you out dancing